P9-CJN-666

Fueling THE FUTURE

Coal

Other books in the Fueling the Future series:

Biomass: Energy from Plants and Animals
Geothermal Power
Hydrogen
Natural Gas
Nuclear Power
Oil
Solar Power
Water
Wind

David M. Haugen, *Book Editor*

Christine Nasso, *Publisher*
Elizabeth Des Chenes, *Managing Editor*

GREENHAVEN PRESS
An imprint of Thomson Gale, a part of The Thomson Corporation

Detroit • New York • San Francisco • New Haven, Conn. • Waterville, Maine • London

For more information, contact
Greenhaven Press
27500 Drake Rd.
Farmington Hills, MI 48331-3535
Or you can visit our Internet site at http://www.gale.com

Articles in Greenhaven Press anthologies are often edited for length to meet page requirements. In addition, original titles of these works are changed to clearly present the main thesis and to explicitly indicate the author's opinion. Every effort is made to ensure that Greenhaven Press accurately reflects the original intent of the authors.

LIBRARY OF CONGRESS CATALOGING-IN-PUBLICATION DATA

Coal / David M. Haugen, book editor.
p. cm. — (Fueling the future)
Includes bibliographical references and index.
ISBN-13: 978-0-7377-3591-8 (hardcover : alk. paper)
ISBN-10: 0-7377-3591-0 (hardcover : alk. paper)
1. Coal. 2. Coal mines and mining. 3. Coal—Analysis. I. Haugen, David M., 1969– .
TP325.C5135 2006
553.2'4—dc22

Printed in the United States of America

Contents

Foreword 8

Introduction 10

Chapter 1: The Mining and Uses of Coal

1. Coal Helped Make the Industrial Revolution Possible 19
   Barbara Freese

   Coal became the energy source used to build and power the steam engines that gave rise to the industrialization of England.

2. How Coal Is Graded and Mined Today 28
   Rita K. Hessley, John W. Reasoner, and John T. Riley

   Various kinds of coal contain different amounts of energy and thus burn more or less efficiently. Coal is either strip-mined or retrieved by excavation

3. The Mining and Uses of Coal 37
   Neil Schlager and Jayne Weisblatt

   Coal is a significant energy source for the production of electricity worldwide, and electricity is essential to modern economies.

Chapter 2: Does Burning Coal Threaten the Environment?

1. Mercury Emissions from Coal Plants Are a Serious Problem 50
   Janet Larsen

   Coal-fired power plants emit mercury, which eventually ends up in America's waterways. People who eat fish exposed to mercury can suffer serious health problems as a result.

2. **Mercury Emissions from Coal Plants Are Not a Serious Problem** 56
Robert Peltier

The health dangers posed by mercury emissions are unproven. Placing tighter controls on U.S. power plants would harm the coal industry without benefiting human health.

3. **The Coal Industry Is Destroying the Environment** 60
Jennifer Hattam

Grassroots organizations in West Virginia warn that the mining industry's destructive practices are spoiling the environment and endangering human health.

Chapter 3: Is Coal the Energy of the Future?

1. **The Pros and Cons of Investing in Clean Coal Technologies** 71
Katie Benner

Environmentalists support investment in new technologies that will reduce coal plant emissions. Critics suggest that these technologies are too expensive and have not been proven to work.

2. **Comparing Coal with Other Energy Sources** 76
Margaret Kriz

When compared with other energy sources, coal is the cheapest and most efficient fuel. Thus, coal will likely remain America's dominant energy source.

3. **Gasification of Coal Will Reduce Pollution Emissions** 89
U.S. Department of Energy
Gasifying coal before it is burned can remove harmful pollutants, making coal a cleaner energy source.

Facts About Coal 94

Glossary 99

Chronology 104

For Further Reading 109

Index 114

Picture Credits 118

About the Editor 119

Foreword

The wind farm at Altamont Pass in northern California epitomizes many people's idea of wind power: Hundreds of towering white turbines generate electricity to power homes, factories, and businesses. The spinning turbine blades call up visions of a brighter future in which clean, renewable energy sources replace dwindling and polluting fossil fuels. The blades also kill over a thousand birds of prey each year. Every energy source, it seems, has its price.

The bird deaths at Altamont Pass make clear an unfortunate fact about all energy sources, including renewables: They have downsides. People want clean, abundant energy to power their modern lifestyles, but few want to pay the costs associated with energy production and use. Oil, coal, and natural gas contain high amounts of energy, but using them produces pollution. Commercial solar energy facilities require hundreds of acres of land and thus must be located in rural areas. Expensive and ugly transmission lines must then be run from the solar plants to the cities that need power. Producing hydrogen for fuel involves the use of dirty fossil fuels, tapping geothermal energy depletes groundwater, and growing biomass for fuel ties up land that could be used to grow food. Hydroelectric power has become increasingly unpopular because dams flood vital habitats and kill wildlife and plants. Perhaps most controversial, nuclear power plants produce highly dangerous radioactive waste. People's reluctance to pay these environmental costs can be seen in the results of a 2006 Center for Economic and Civic Opinion poll. When asked how much they would support a power plant in their neighborhood, 66 percent of respondents said they would oppose it.

Many scientists warn that fossil fuel use creates emissions that threaten human health and cause global warming. Moreover, numerous scientists claim that fossil fuels are running out. As a result of these concerns, many nations have begun to revisit the energy sources that first powered human enterprises. In his 2006 State of the Union speech, U.S. president George W. Bush announced that since 2001 the United States has spent "$10 billion to develop cleaner, cheaper, and more reliable alternative energy sources," such as biomass and wind power. Despite Bush's positive rhetoric, many critics contend that the renewable energy sources he refers to are still as inefficient as they ever were and cannot possibly power modern economies. As Jerry Taylor and Peter Van Doren of the Cato Institute note, "The market share for nonhydro renewable energy . . . has languished between 1 and 3 percent for decades." Controversies such as this have been a constant throughout the history of humanity's search for the perfect energy source.

Greenhaven Press's Fueling the Future series explores this history. Each volume in the series traces the development of one energy source, and investigates the controversies surrounding its environmental impact and its potential to power humanity's future. The anthologies provide a variety of selections written by scientists, environmental activists, industry leaders, and government experts. Volumes also contain useful research tools, including an introductory essay providing important context, and an annotated table of contents that enables students to locate selections of interest easily. In addition, each volume includes an index, chronology, bibliography, glossary, and a Facts About section, which lists useful information about each energy source. Other features include numerous charts, graphs, and cartoons, which offer additional avenues for learning important information about the topic.

Fueling the Future volumes provide students with important resources for learning about the energy sources upon which human societies depend. Although it is easy to take energy for granted in developed nations, this series emphasizes how energy sources are also problematic. The U.S. Energy Information Administration calls energy "essential to life." Whether scientists will be able to develop the energy sources necessary to sustain modern life is the vital question explored in Greenhaven Press's Fueling the Future series.

Introduction

"Coal may in fact be the most useful mineral, second only to food and water as a necessity of life."

—Rita K. Hessley, John W. Reasoner, and John T. Riley, *Coal Science*

"While coal makes an important contribution to economic and social development worldwide, its environmental impact has been a challenge."

—World Coal Institute, *The Coal Resource*

The use of the black organic sediment known as coal dates back at least fifteen centuries, when Roman soldiers occupying Britain found that the mineral could be burned to provide heat to ward off the cold. Since that time, coal energy has had many uses. In the eighteenth century coal replaced wood-based charcoal as the prime smelting agent to make cast iron. In the 1770s coal powered the steam engines that made possible the Industrial Revolution. It also was used to power trains and thus drove the expansion of railroads in the nineteenth century. Coal continued to fill the residential fireplaces of industrializing nations through the early twentieth century, but its use as a home heating source dwindled as its importance to commercial industry rose. It was the advent of electricity in the late 1870s that revealed coal's lasting relevance to the modern world. Coal quickly became—and remains—a dominant fuel for providing electricity worldwide. Despite the world's reliance on coal, people around the world worry about coal's impact on the environment. As coal usage expands, these concerns only intensify.

The United States Depends Heavily on Coal

In the United States today more than 1.1 billion tons of coal are consumed annually. Ninety-two percent of this total is utilized in the production of electricity. The remaining percentage is used in the smelting of steel, as well as for other industrial applications and home heating. Nearly half of U.S. electricity needs are met by coal-fired power plants, around 20 percent is supplied by nuclear power, natural gas accounts for about 18 percent, while oil and alternative energies constitute the remainder. Coal consumption in the United States is high because the nation has vast coal reserves (perhaps more than one-third of the world's total), and this abundance has kept the price of coal low in comparison with other energy sources. The United States exports

In the 19th century coal was used to power steam locomotives, such as this one. Passengers rode in stagecoaches that were pulled by the locomotive.

Where Is Coal Located in the United States?

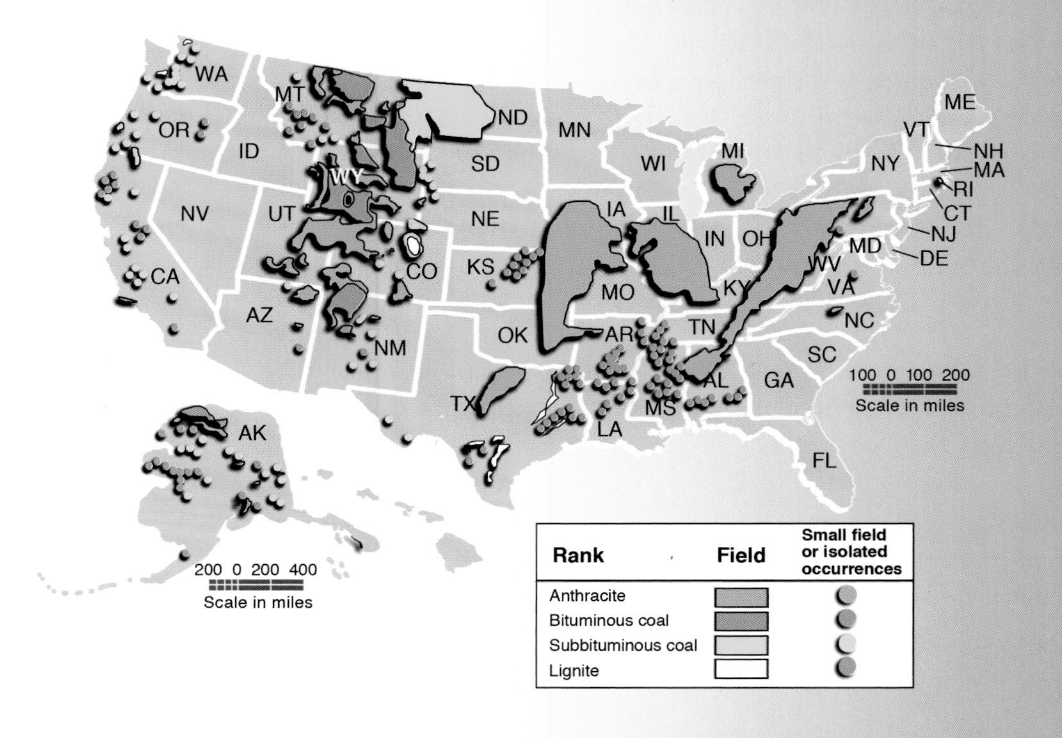

Source: U.S. Department of Energy, Energy Information Administration, *U.S. Coal Reserves: 1997 Update*, 1999, http://www.eia.doe.gov/cneaf/coal/reserves/chapter1.html#fig1.

huge quantities of coal, which—coupled with the exports of other large coal-rich countries—has ensured that coal remains a cheap and reliable energy source throughout the globe.

Despite coal's appeal as an energy source, its use has serious environmental drawbacks. Burning coal produces carbon dioxide (CO_2), a greenhouse gas that has been linked to global warming. Coal emissions also include nitrogen oxide, sulfur dioxide, and mercury—all of which pose health threats to humans and wildlife, according to many experts. Coal is not alone in its production of dangerous emissions, of course; all fossil fuels emit carbon dioxide and other pollutants when burned.

Indeed, the burning of oil—mainly in the form of automotive gasoline—is responsible for the largest share of greenhouse gas emissions. Coal's pollutants, however, are still a major concern. In fact, the growing demand for electricity in developing countries has many analysts concerned that coal emissions will steadily increase. In 2003 the International Energy Agency (IEA) noted that China's rapid industrialization increased energy demands by 14 percent, much of which was met with rising coal consumption. Increases in global population also strain energy supplies. The IEA predicts that over the next thirty years, world energy demands will expand by 60 percent, and two-thirds of the increase will occur in developing nations. In 2005 Roger Wicks, head of the World Coal Institute, remarked, "Not surprisingly, this outlook carries with it a heavy CO_2 burden. . . . In

Although coal is a vital energy source, its excavation causes great environmental damage. Pictured are tailings piles that result when coal is mined from within the earth.

Burning coal releases carbon dioxide (CO_2) into the earth's atmosphere. Carbon dioxide is believed to be a cause of global warming.

2002, coal accounted for some 38% of world energy-related CO_2 emissions. The increase in CO_2 over the next 30 years mirrors the primary-energy demand increase—around 60%."

The pollution caused by burning coal has dogged its use from early times. In the late thirteenth century Londoners were so overwhelmed by coal smoke that King Edward I was compelled to issue a ban on the burning of coal. However, then—as now—the fuel's abundance and usefulness in meeting the energy needs for an ever-expanding population ensured its continued use. It was not until the late 1960s that coal's potentially dangerous emissions became the target of an environmental backlash. With the rise of ecology movements throughout industrial nations, pollution became an urgent issue, and environmentalists began calling for an end to coal use. In response, electric utilities turned to nuclear power to meet increasing energy needs, thus avoiding the need to build more coal-fired plants. Moreover, the newly formed U.S. Environmental Protection Agency passed laws regulating power plant emissions. The law that had the most impact on the coal industry was the 1970 Clean Air Act, which aimed to improve air quality by reducing the amount of harmful emissions produced by fossil fuel and chemical polluters. The Clean Air Act has been amended and strengthened over subsequent decades to address carbon dioxide, sulfur dioxide, nitrogen oxide, and mercury emissions as each of these threats took prominence at various times in the late twentieth century.

The Coal Industry Responds to Environmental Concerns

Faced with EPA regulations, the coal-power industry was forced to reduce emissions. The installation of "scrubbers" in coal plants' exhaust systems has significantly cut sulfur dioxide released into the air. Smokestack filters have reduced particulate matter, and improved burning processes have lessened the problem of nitrogen oxide pollution. Such fixes have been relatively inexpensive and do not require complete revamping of plant design. Carbon dioxide emissions, however, have yet to be so cheaply and easily remedied. In 1997 a world summit was held in Kyoto, Japan, to devise ways to reduce carbon dioxide emissions and slow global warming. The resulting Kyoto Protocol, which went into effect in 2005, required developed nations to reduce CO_2 output by 5 percent between 2008 and 2012. The agreement was historic because it showed a worldwide willingness to transition from fossil fuels to cleaner renewables. The United States, however, did not ratify the protocol—and thus abide by its terms—thanks in large part to the lobbying of the coal industry. Still, the U.S. government, under the administration of George W. Bush, is working to reduce greenhouse gas

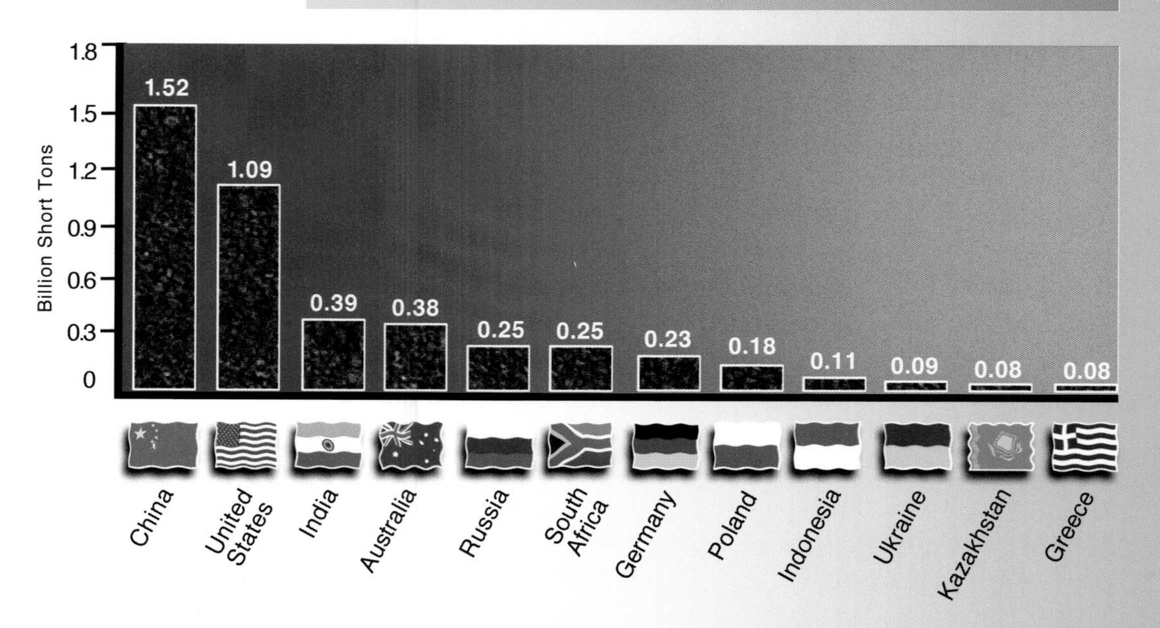

Source: "World Coal Production: Top Producing Countries, 2002," in *Annual Energy Review 2003*, U.S. Department of Energy, Energy Information Administration, Office of Energy Markets and End Use, September 7, 2004. http://www.eia.doe.gov/emeu/aer/pdf/aer.pdf.

emissions. The Clean Coal Power Initiative (CCPI) was launched in 2002 and is rewarding the coal industry for experimenting with new, clean coal technologies that significantly reduce carbon emissions. The aim of the CCPI is to keep coal a mainstay of American power at a time when environmental priorities favor alternative energy programs.

Coal Will Continue to Be a Staple Energy Source

The emphasis on improving coal technologies and reducing pollutants reveals that the world is far from dispensing with this fossil fuel. In fact, coal has remained a valued commodity even as the world has become more concerned about the environment. In the United States, demand for coal power has not significantly diminished since 1960. With the public hesitant to expand nuclear energy and with alternative energy development still its infancy, America is planning what in the heyday of the 1970s environmental movement seemed inconceivable—the building of around one hundred new coal plants across the country. As Simon Romero of the *New York Times* noted in a 2004 article, "Altogether, energy companies in the United States have announced plans to build more coal-fired power plants in the last 12 months than they did in the last 12 years." Part of the boom is due to expected rises in natural gas prices and part is due to the promise of clean coal technologies. Even if new coal plants are more efficient and more ecologically sound, however, the overall increase in coal burning may have negative consequences for the environment and human health, many experts warn.

America is not alone in addressing the challenges of continued reliance on coal. Because coal is relatively plentiful and cheap, China, India, and a host of developing nations view it as the key to economic growth. The majority of coal pollutants in the twenty-first century, then, may come not from the industrialized West but from East Asia and the globalizing nations of Africa. This fact will likely not deter its use in the coming years, but it may help speed the global application of clean coal technologies. As the World Coal Institute concludes, "Demand for coal and its vital role in the world's energy system is set to continue." Whether the world can balance the energy benefits of coal with its environmental impact is yet to be determined.

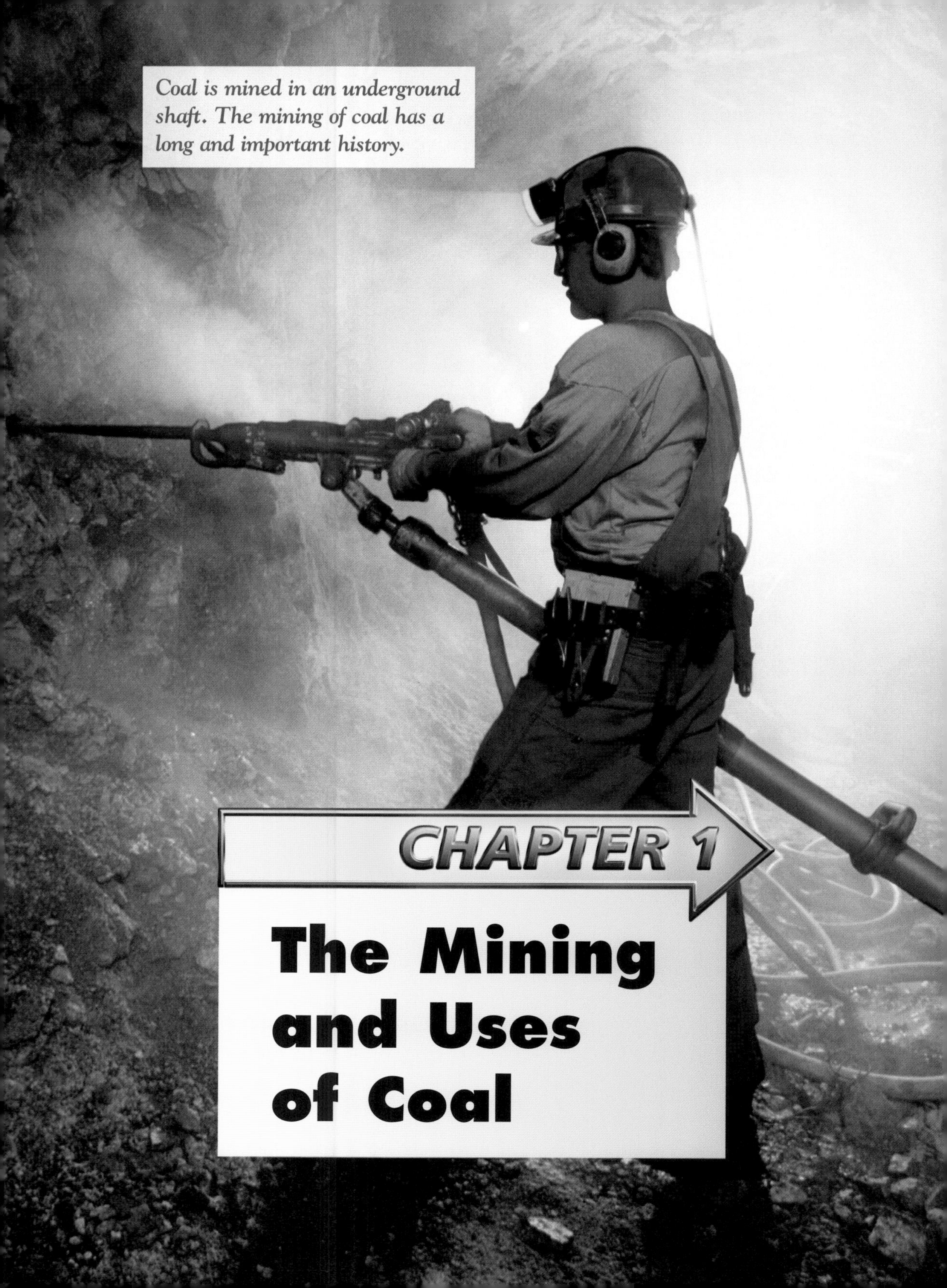

Coal is mined in an underground shaft. The mining of coal has a long and important history.

CHAPTER 1

The Mining and Uses of Coal

Coal Helped Make the Industrial Revolution Possible

Barbara Freese

Barbara Freese is a former assistant attorney general in Minnesota; she focused on environmental law. In the following selection from her book *Coal: A Human History*, Freese explains how James Watt's invention of the steam engine in the 1770s gave rise to the industrialization of England. According to Freese, Watt's engines provided the nation with the power to industrialize, but Britain still needed iron to build the engines and required factories to house them. Most iron works used wood charcoal to smelt iron, but England's wood supply was dwindling. The solution to this problem came in the 1780s, when the iron industry began using purified coal, or coke, as a smelting agent in iron production. Fortunately, the island nation had plenty of coal reserves to feed its iron industry. As Freese writes, for the next fifty years, coal powered England's factories. Soon the rest of Europe and America would follow England's lead as the Industrial Revolution transformed the Western world.

James Watt, the son of a carpenter, was born in Scotland in 1736. . . . [As a school boy] Watt thrived in mathematics . . . and studied the art of making mathematical instruments. It was in this capacity that he was asked in his late twenties to fix a

Barbara Freese, *Coal: A Human History*. New York: Perseus, 2003.

small model of a Newcomen engine [an early eighteenth-century engine that used atmospheric pressure to drive a piston] kept at Glasgow University.

Watt's Idea

Like the larger version, the model was extremely wasteful, needing lots of coal to keep it going. Watt realized that as steam was injected and then cooled with water, heat was wasted in the constant reheating and cooling of the [piston] cylinder. As Watt later told it, he was walking through a park in Glasgow one day when the solution suddenly flashed into his mind: He

Eighteenth century inventor James Watt experimented with ways to improve the steam engine.

would install a separate condenser [where steam was condensed into water]. That is, the cylinder would be attached to another container that was immersed in cold water and thus kept cool. After the cylinder filled with steam, the steam would pass into this cooler container, where it would condense. In this way, the cylinder itself would always stay hot, and ready for the next injection of steam. According to a good friend of Watt's, "this capital improvement flashed upon his mind at once, and filled him with rapture."

But turning his rapture-inducing idea into a working steam engine would prove to be an ordeal. Watt found a patron in a local industrialist who was having trouble keeping his coal mines dry [from underground floodwater] with his Newcomen engine, and who hired Watt to improve it. Years went by, but lacking mechanics skilled enough to craft the parts he needed, Watt could not build a successful engine. At one point in the midst of all these years of failure, Watt gloomily concluded that "of all things in life, there is nothing more foolish than inventing," and he repeatedly swore to give the whole thing up.

A New, Improved Engine

Then Watt found a new partner, the irrepressible Birmingham industrialist Matthew Boulton, and one of the most celebrated business partnerships in history was launched. Boulton was more than a manufacturer; he was an industrial visionary who had surrounded himself with people who shared his fascination with technology and his faith in how it could transform the world. . . .

Boulton had a longstanding interest in steam engines, in part because the water wheels that powered Soho [his craft goods factory] were unreliable. He had earlier performed his own unsuccessful experiments with the steam engine, and he even corresponded with his friend Benjamin Franklin on engine design. Boulton knew of Watt's work in Scotland, and decided to back him. Watt moved to Birmingham and began working on his engine at Soho in 1773. With the skilled workers, financial backing, and emotional encouragement Boulton provided, Watt was able to build a working engine. The all-important cylinder had been crafted by the pioneering iron founder, John Wilkinson.

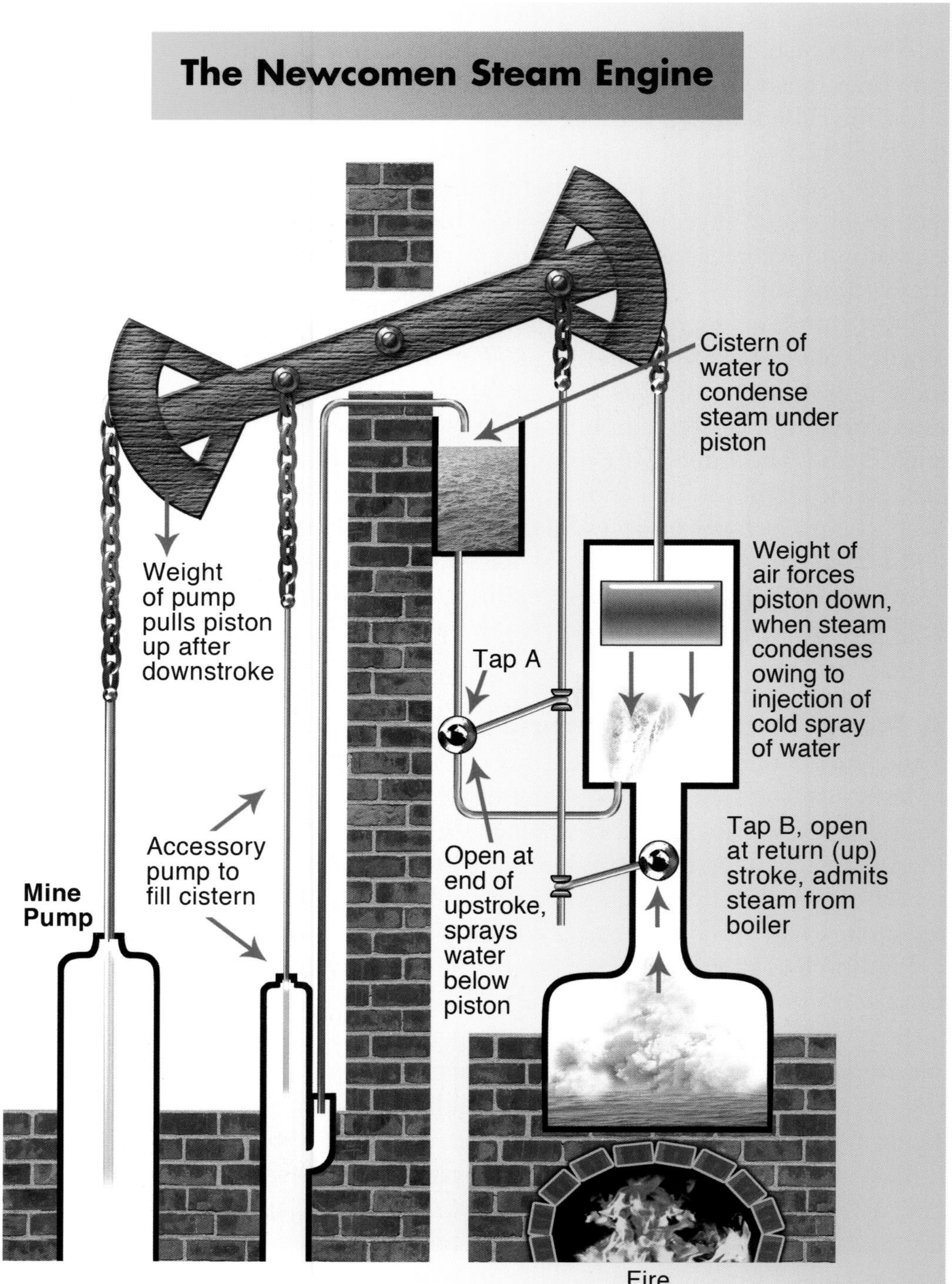

The Newcomen Steam Engine

Cistern of water to condense steam under piston

Weight of pump pulls piston up after downstroke

Tap A

Weight of air forces piston down, when steam condenses owing to injection of cold spray of water

Accessory pump to fill cistern

Mine Pump

Open at end of upstroke, sprays water below piston

Tap B, open at return (up) stroke, admits steam from boiler

Fire

The Watt Steam Pump

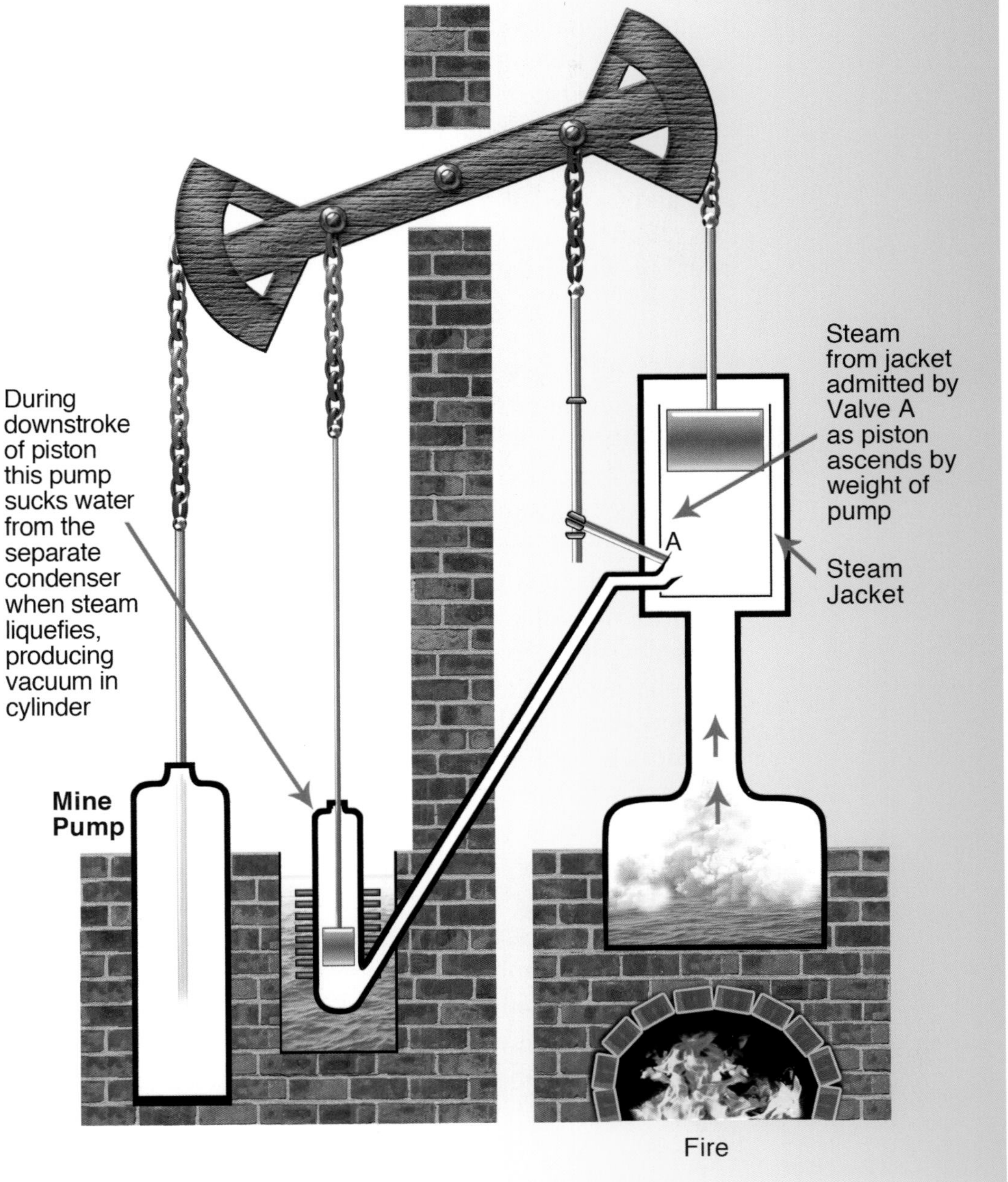

Steam from jacket admitted by Valve A as piston ascends by weight of pump

During downstroke of piston this pump sucks water from the separate condenser when steam liquefies, producing vacuum in cylinder

A

Steam Jacket

Mine Pump

Fire

In 1776, as the revolutionary events in the American colonies were unfolding, James Watt put his first two revolutionary engines to work, one to pump water in a coal mine and one to blow the bellows in Wilkinson's iron foundry.

Although Watt improved the steam engine in myriad ways, his greatest achievement was in getting Newcomen's device to squeeze four times more motive force out of a lump of coal. The steam engine's new fuel efficiency allowed it to leave the coal mines and at last find a welcome in the nation's factories. Watt and Boulton marketed their product as an energy-efficiency device and took their royalties as a cut of the estimated coal savings. Watt would become a national legend, and his engine would be widely hailed as a boon to all humanity. . . .

England's New Power Supply

With its coal and its steam engines, Britain had plenty of power, but its ability to take advantage of that power depended on having the iron needed to build the engines and the factories. This was a major constraint, because at the beginning of the industrial revolution, iron was still essentially a forest product; you couldn't make it without burning vast amounts of wood, which Britain simply didn't have. Since ancient times, iron had been smelted with charcoal, which would be mixed in direct contact with the iron ore and then fired. Charcoal provided not only the necessary heat but also the carbon needed to promote the chemical reduction of the iron (the oxides in the ore would combine with the carbon and be released as carbon dioxide).

Ironworks were notorious for their rapacious consumption of wood fuel, and they were often forced to move to new locations when they had depleted the local supply. The logical solution, of course, was to start smelting iron with coal instead of wood, but there was a problem: Impurities in the coal would contaminate the iron when the coal and iron ore were mixed together. As a result, long after other fuel-intensive industries had turned to coal, the iron industry was still gulping down great tracts of woodland, and domestic iron production was stifled by high fuel costs. . . .

The key to making usable iron with coal was to first bake the coal to drive off the volatiles and turn it into "coke," much the way wood is turned into charcoal. It took a century of experimentation with coke before it was successfully used in the early 1700s to make cast iron (iron that is melted and then poured into pre-made casts). But most of the demand was for wrought iron (iron beaten into shape while malleable). It was not until the mid-1780s that the technology had advanced enough to allow the industry to use coke for all stages of iron production, both cast and wrought. Britain had taken another major step out of the woods.

England's Industry Grows

Iron production came to depend on coal in another way. Before steam, iron furnaces were kept burning by water; that is, the blast of air needed to keep the fire sufficiently hot was provided by waterwheels. The limited force of the water power (and the fact that charcoal would crumble from the weight of the ore if the furnace was too large) kept iron works relatively small, and they often had to shut down in the summer when the streams fell too low. With steam engines to provide a bigger blast and an ample supply of coke to fuel the process, blast furnaces grew much larger, and were able to pour out lots of inexpensive iron all year long. Instead of being dependent on imported iron, Britain became the world's most efficient iron producer in just a few years. The nation finally had the cheap and ample supply of iron it needed to build its industries at home, and its empire abroad.

Now that iron could be made with coal, a critical organic constraint on the growth of the industrial economy had fallen away. The production of coal, steam engines, and iron spiraled upward at a pace that would have made [British economist] Adam Smith dizzy, and it was accelerated by the mutually reinforcing relationships

FACTS TO CONSIDER

Coal Use Expands in the Sixteenth Century

From the sixteenth century on, "various industrial processes—baking, brewing, glass manufacture, and so on—were adapted to the use of coal, either in its raw form or as coke, and the increasing prevalence of chimneys made coal more acceptable as a domestic fuel."

A.R. Griffin, *Coalmining*, 1971.

James Watt's improved steam engine. Watt's invention increased the demand for coal and propelled the industrial revolution forward.

that existed among the three. Steam increased the demand for both coal and iron, and also made coal and iron easier and cheaper to produce. Cheaper coal and iron made steam engines cheaper to build and to run, which, in turn, attracted more people to steam power, further increasing the demand for coal and iron, and so on.

The nation's coal industry had already grown relatively large by 1700 just by meeting the domestic and non-iron industrial needs of the nation, but it would expand tenfold by 1830, and double again by 1854. The nation raced to open new coal mines to meet the skyrocketing demand. Between 1842 and 1856 the number of coal mines quadrupled. Coal had completely permeated society. It was not only directly present in the bellies of the steam engines, but indirectly present in the engines' iron cylinders and pistons, in the loom's iron frames, in the factories' iron girders, and later in the iron railroads, bridges, and steamships that would define the industrial age.

The Factory Boom

Steam power did not create the factory system, but it irreversibly changed the scale, the nature, and the location of industrial enterprise. Early factories, mainly cotton mills, were powered by waterwheels, a technology that had been widely used in Britain and elsewhere since ancient times. (So close was the association between factories and water power that factories were still commonly known as "mills" long into the steam age.) As long as the industrialization of Britain was powered by water, though, it would go only so fast. . . .

Coal spawned much larger and ever more mechanized factories because the power available from underground was so much greater than that supplied by a waterwheel. And, because its energy had already been handily condensed over millions of years, coal concentrated the factories and workforces in urban areas instead of dispersing them throughout the countryside. In short, coal allowed the industrialization of Britain to gain a momentum that was nothing short of revolutionary.

The Industrial Revolution

In its impact on humankind, the industrial revolution has been compared to the discovery of fire, to the invention of the wheel, and to tasting the apple from the Tree of Knowledge. The term *industrial revolution* falls in and out of fashion, but whatever you call it, something transformative took hold in Britain between about 1780 and 1830. From this point on, means of production would grow larger and more mechanized as factories replaced handicraft industries. People would move to the cities in droves and into ever larger workforces. Markets would become increasingly global, and for many, material wealth would reach undreamed of heights.

How Coal Is Graded and Mined Today

Rita K. Hessley, John W. Reasoner, and John T. Riley

In the first part of the following selection Rita K. Hessley, John W. Reasoner, and John T. Riley explain how different kinds of coal are characterized. Coal type depends upon the kinds of plants that formed it and the environmental conditions that prevailed at the time the coal formed. Coal rank refers to the amount of pressure and heat the plant and animal material underwent as it was turned into coal. Finally, coal grade refers to the level of impurities coal contains. Hessley, Reasoner, and Riley also explain how coal is mined in modern times. According to them, strip-mining and underground mining are the two main methods. Strip-mining is most efficient, but it causes extensive environmental damage. Underground mining also poses problems such as cave-ins. Hessley is a professor of chemical technology at the University of Cincinnati in Ohio. Reasoner and Riley are professors of chemistry at Western Kentucky University in Bowling Green. Reasoner is now retired.

Coal deposits were formed over the course of thousands of years through the alternating processes of land elevation, plant growth and decay, and land subsidence. Because of this, coal is a highly variable and heterogeneous material. In one coal deposit in Nova Scotia, for instance, 68 levels of different plant types have been found across a 1,400-ft seam. It is true that all

Rita K. Hessley, John W. Reasoner, and John T. Riley, *Coal Science: An Introduction to Chemistry, Technology, and Utilization*. Hoboken, NJ: John Wiley & Sons, 1986.

coal has essentially a common origin, and basically the same components in varying proportions, but it is not true that [as one 1978 coal reference book stated] "coal is coal and nature has created no particular kinds." Substantial and significant differences in coal samples can be measured. Ultimately, coal is not all the same. From the earliest industrial times it has been important to classify coal in descriptive categories. Unfortunately, a number of different systems have evolved together, and they are not unequivocal. However, some generally recognized and accepted terms are in use throughout the coal industry. . . .

Type and Rank of Coal

Type, rank, and *grade* are three terms that describe particular characteristics of coal. The kinds of plant material from which a coal originated, the kinds of mineral inclusions, and the

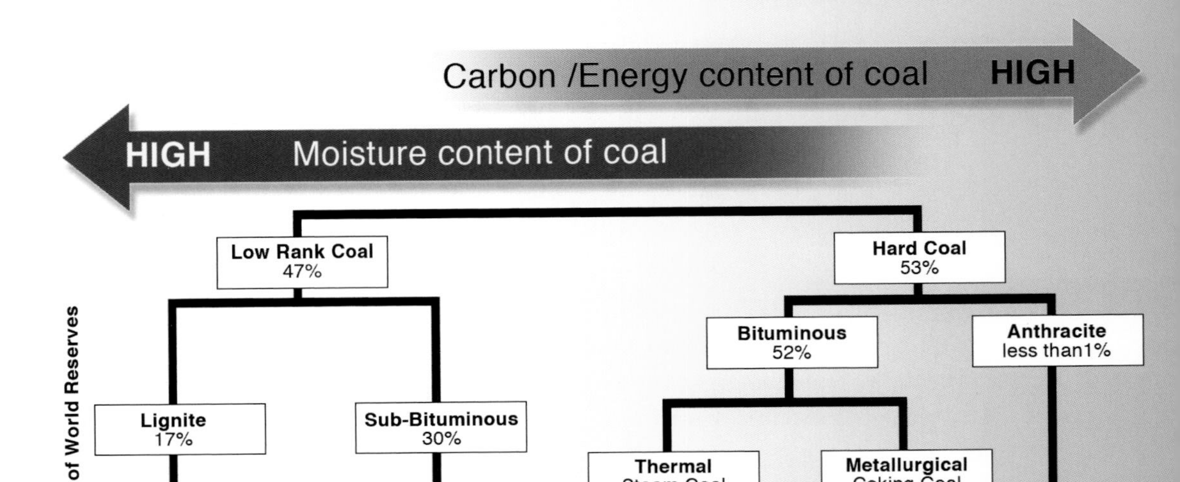

Source: World Coal Institute, *The Coal Resource*. London: World Coal Institute, May 2005.

nature of biochemical reaction conditions that prevailed during periods of plant decay give rise to coal types. The two main types of coal are banded and nonbanded. As the name indicates, banded coal consists of discrete layers or bands composed in part of the remains of woody plant tissues, fine plant debris, and "mineral charcoal" or fusain. Smoother and more finely grained coals derived primarily from spores and algae constitute non-banded coal.

The rank to which a coal is assigned refers to the extent of metamorphosis the deposited plant and animal matter has undergone. The pressure and heat caused by protracted periods of burial or by the folding of the earth's crust brought about progressive changes in the structure of the organic material as it was converted into coal. Coal that has undergone the most ex-

Not all coal is the same. Coal differs depending on what kind of plant material, minerals, and biochemical reactions helped it form.

tensive change, or metamorphosis, has the highest rank. Chemical analyses are carried out to determine the degree of metamorphosis in a sample. In practice, the rank of a coal is assigned according to its fixed carbon value or its heating value. The fixed carbon value is obtained by subtracting the moisture, ash and volatile matter from 100. Ash is the residue that remains after combustion of a coal sample, and volatile matter is the material driven off by heating a coal sample in the absence of air in a special furnace under prescribed conditions. Volatile matter includes all the gases, other than water vapor, that are evolved under the conditions of the test. It has been found that the process of coalification increases the amount of fixed carbon and generally decreases the amount of moisture and the amount of volatile matter found in coal. The coalification series begins with lignite as the lowest-rank coal and progresses with gradual changes in fixed carbon and volatile matter to anthracite, or hard coal, which has the highest rank. . . .

Although all coal, even at the highest rank, contains moisture, the amount of moisture in a sample of coal is extremely important to its value to virtually every user. First, for every unit weight of water in a shipment of coal, less coal is being received. Since the price is paid per total unit (usually per ton) of material, the presence of more than a small percentage of moisture in coal from a particular area renders it of less commercial value. Second, once coal is ignited, the amount of heat it gives off also determines its relative value for uses ranging from domestic heating fuel to boiler fuel in steel or power production. The conversion of water from a liquid to a vapor requires a substantial amount of heat—heat that is "stolen" from the coal itself, again diminishing its value as a fuel. The heat content, calorific value, or energy value of coal can be determined in a laboratory test and is recorded in British thermal units (Btu). One Btu is the amount of heat required to raise the temperature of 1 lb of water 1° F. As the rank of coal increases, so does the ratio of fixed carbon to moisture, and the potential heat content, or energy value, of the coal. . . . The highest-rank anthracite coals have somewhat less heating value than do the medium- and low-volatile bituminous coals. This illustrates the complex chemical nature of coal and shows that, while the amount of fixed carbon may be used to establish the rank of a coal, the amount of volatile matter and moisture cannot be overlooked.

Coal Grades

The grade of a coal refers to the amount and the kind of inorganic mineral impurities found bound into the coal. Among a variety of inorganic components, sulfur is perhaps the most significant. It interferes with catalytic materials used in coal conversion processes and is converted to gaseous sulfur dioxide, SO_2, a toxic and corrosive pollutant, when coal is burned. Although the kinds and amounts of inorganic components are becoming increasingly critical as ecological and environmental considerations, the rank to which a coal belongs is more frequently referred to than its grade in general discussions.

Before leaving this topic of the character and value of coal, mention should be made of the coal identified as "meta-anthracite". . . . Meta-anthracite, sometimes called superanthracite in older texts, is organic material that has metamorphosized almost completely to graphite. It is not found in many locations and, because it has a diminished heat content, is not a very valuable coal. The Narragansett Basin region of Rhode Island and Massachussetts contains an extensive field of meta-anthracite, probably the only such deposit in the United States. . . .

Mining Operations

In 1929 it was foreseen that advances in technology would make coal mining an art. Certainly, mining then was a simple matter of applying sufficient labor to the effort once the geologic, geographic, and economic considerations regarding the feasibility of the mining operation had been dealt with. Because of increased sophistication brought about by recent technology, modern coal mining may be considered simple because it requires less raw human physical exertion, but modern equipment is not particularly simple. Besides being an art, mining is now also an extremely complex business operation.

Basically, what has not changed [since 1929] are the two principal mining methods: strip, or "open work," mining and underground, or "closed work," mining.

Coal Mining Methods

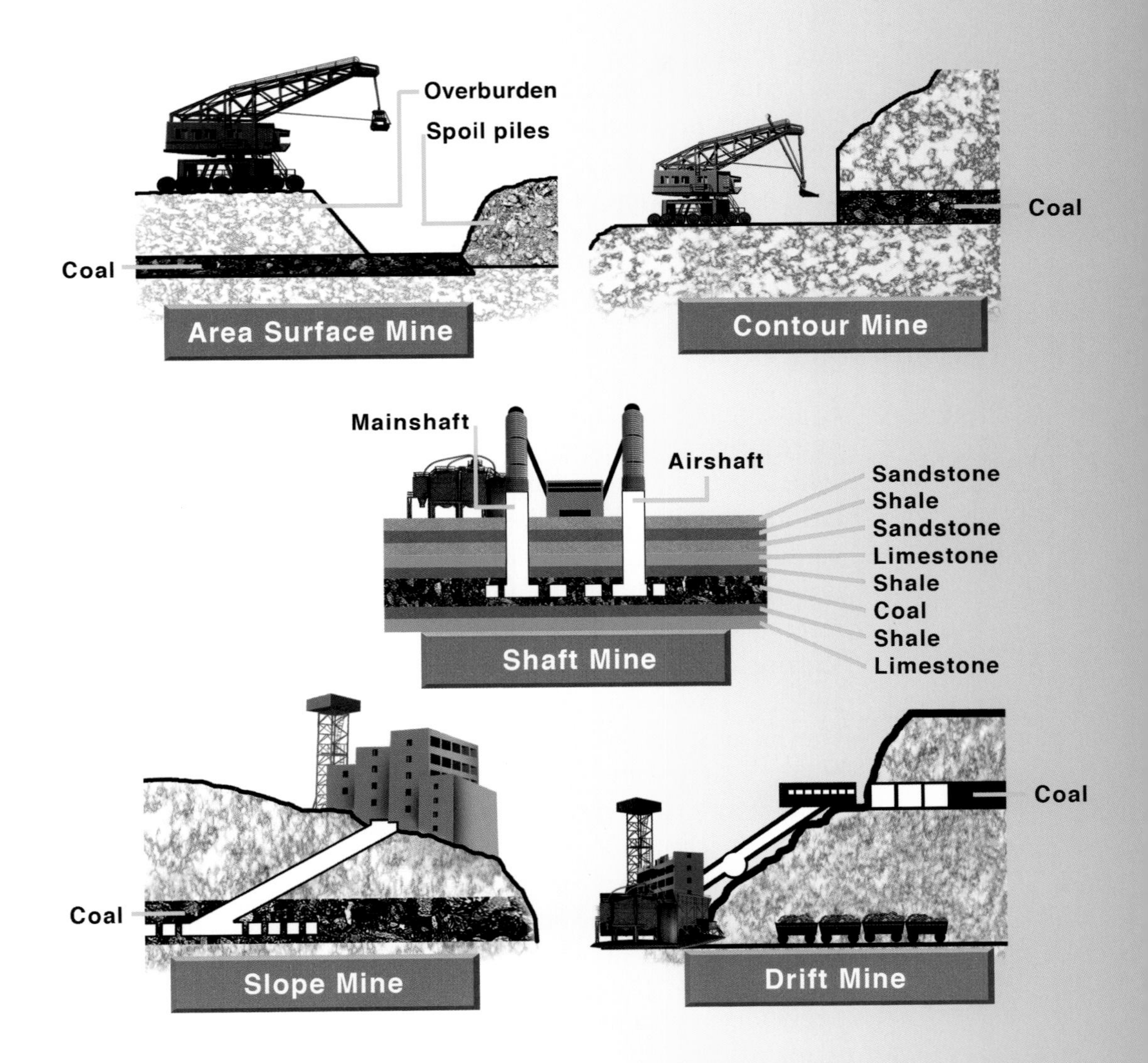

Source: U.S. Department of Energy, Energy Information Administration, *Coal Data: A Reference*, February 1995, http://tonto.eia.doe.gov/FTPROOT/Coal/006493.pdf.

Strip mining is the simplest operation. The overburden [top level of soil and rock] is removed, and the coal is dug, loaded, and hauled away. . . . Strip mining is becoming increasingly more economical, more rapid, and safer than underground methods, but even with modern equipment, the character of the overburden is important and may limit the feasibility of strip mining. In general, the rate at which the overburden is removed is determined by whether it consists largely of loose soil and shale, or whether substantial rock beds require preliminary blasting. Because of the attractiveness of strip mining, even relatively thick layers of overburden are removed if the underlying coal seam is evaluated as warranting such a measure. . . .

By numbers, the advantages of strip mining surpass its disadvantages. Among its advantages are (1) more of the coal is removed; (2) less labor is required per ton produced, and the miners require less training and experience; (3) no timbering is required; (4) larger hauling units can be employed; (5) it is more rapid; (6) equipment can be moved to subsequent sites or sold; and (7) danger to miners in the form of poor mine ventilation and mine roof collapse is eliminated. The primary disadvantage from the production point of view is that weather conditions can limit or eliminate mining operations for lengthy intervals, causing substantial financial losses. The extensive scarring of the land caused by destruction of all the vegetation and soil is a disadvantage of considerable and growing concern. For the most part, with no externally applied pressure to do otherwise, strip mining sites have been abandoned with only minimal effort to restore the land. Recent public awareness has resulted in legislation requiring that various specific efforts be made by coal companies to reclaim depleted mine sites and restore them to conditions that will again permit plant growth and support animal life. This topic is the subject of ongoing debate and controversy.

Underground Mining

The oldest underground mining method is termed conventional, or room and pillar. This was the first and is the most complicated mining method ever used. It consists of working

Underground mining techniques are used in Wyoming at the Black Thunder Coal Mine, one of the largest coal mines in the United States.

out rooms and leaving behind coal pillars to support the ceiling. In addition to the main ventilation and access shafts, a maze-like series of arteries is cut into the seam. The pattern of rooms and pillars is developed according to a definite, well-planned system. Laws govern the minimum size of the pillars and the maximum number of rooms allowed in a seam. Obviously, roof control is critical, and fatal cave-ins occur. Although considerable mechanical innovation has been applied to this method, the use of pillars of coal still results in the inability to remove 35–70% of the available coal. Some or all may be removed in a later operation, called robbing pillars, in which an intentional, controlled cave-in is caused. The average recovery of the coal using this two-stage process is 80%.

The longwall method, used for many years in Europe and

becoming more common in the United States, involves the use of a mechanical self-advancing roof. Rather than cutting the coal face to leave pillars supporting the ceiling, movable steel beams are attached to a shearing mechanism. As the coal is shaved away and falls to a conveyor, the unit moves forward, allowing the unsupported ceiling behind it to collapse in a controlled and uniform manner. As much as 90% of the coal is recovered using this method. It is certainly a more rapid and simpler method than room and pillar. . . .

A continuous miner is another excavating device used in underground mining. It has a front cutting head consisting of several continuously revolving chains carrying cutters or picks. The unit is mounted on caterpillar treads and uses a conveyor belt to move coal away from the face to shuttle cars following the unit. This device can cut an entry 12–20 ft wide and up to 8 ft high.

The Mining and Uses of Coal

Neil Schlager and Jayne Weisblatt

In the following selection Neil Schlager and Jayne Weisblatt describe several modern uses for coal energy. As the authors state, coal is a significant energy source for the production of electricity worldwide, and electricity is essential to modern economies. The authors also note that coal is used in the production of steel and cement, two other elements necessary for economic development. Neil Schlager and Jayne Weisblatt are freelance writers and editors.

Coal supplies about one-fourth of the world's energy needs. Coal is a solid hydrocarbon made primarily of carbon and hydrogen with small amounts of other elements such as sulfur and nitrogen. Coal looks like black rock, and it leaves black dust on things that it touches.

Origins of Coal

Millions of years ago earth was covered with swamps full of giant trees and other plants. When they died, these trees fell into the swampy water and were gradually covered by other plants and soil. All living things, including plants and animals, are composed mainly of carbon. Over millions of years, the carbon in the swamp plants was compressed and heated. This caused it to rot, exactly the way fruit and vegetables rot if kept too long. This rotting produced methane gas, also known as swamp gas.

Over several thousand years, the weight of the upper layers

Neil Schlager and Jayne Weisblatt, eds., "Fossil Fuels," from *Alternative Energy*, vol. 1. Detroit: Thomson Gale. Reprinted with permission.

compacted the lower layers into a substance called peat. Peat is the first step on the way to the formation of coal and other fuels. People can use peat as fuel simply by cutting chunks of it out of the ground and burning them. Ireland used to be covered with peat, which was the main source of fuel there for years. The Great Dismal Swamp in North Carolina and Virginia contains almost one billion tons of peat.

As the peat continued to be compacted by new layers of dead plants, it became hotter. . . . The heat and pressure gradually turned it into coal. Most of the earth's coal was formed during one of two periods: the Carboniferous (360 million–290 million years ago) or the Tertiary (65 million–1.6 million years ago).

Finding Coal

There are large reserves of coal all over the world. China has nearly one-half of the world's coal reserves and produces nearly one-fourth of the coal that is used every year. There are also large reserves of coal in North America, India, and central Asia. In the United States, most coal comes from mines in Montana, North Dakota, Wyoming, Alaska, Illinois, and Colorado. There are also coal deposits in the Appalachian area, especially in West Virginia and Pennsylvania.

Getting Coal Out of the Ground

Coal is extracted from the earth through mining techniques that vary depending on where the coal is located. If a coal seam (or deposit) is deep below the surface of the earth, miners use subsurface mining. They dig vertical tunnels into the ground to reach the seam and then dig horizontal tunnels at the level of the seam. The miners ride elevators down to the seam, dig out the coal, and transport it back up to the surface. To prevent the earth from collapsing, miners leave pillars of coal standing to hold up the tunnel roof. Despite this precaution, coal mines sometimes collapse, killing miners trapped inside.

Surface mining, or strip mining, is a process of taking coal off the surface of the earth without going underground. Miners use giant shovels to remove dirt, called overburden, from the coal seam and then use explosives to blast the coal out of the rock. Strip mining is much safer than subsurface mining, but it leaves huge scars on the land and can contribute to water pollution.

Making Coal Useful

Coal comes out of the ground in chunks up to 3 or 4 feet (0.9–1.2 meters) across, and coal processors crush it into chunks about the size of a person's fist. These chunks of coal then go through a screen that separates out the smallest pieces. Coal plants sometimes clean coal by setting it, which washes out the heavier particles of stone. The plant may then dry the coal to make it lighter and help it burn better. Once processing is complete, coal is transported to buyers using trains, barges (flat cargo-carrying boats), and trucks.

Coal comes in several types, depending on how pure the carbon [content] is, which also corresponds to how old the coal is. Coal is rated by heat value (how much heat it can produce when it burns). The purer the carbon [content] is, the higher the heat value. Heat value is measured in British thermal units, or Btu, per pound. A Btu is the amount of heat required to raise the temperature of one pound of water one degree Fahrenheit.

- Anthracite (AN-thruh-syte) contains between 86 and 98 percent pure carbon and has a heat value of 13,500 to 15,600 Btu per pound.
- Bituminous (bye-TOO-muh-nuhs) coal contains between 60 and 86 percent pure carbon and has a heat value of 8,300 to 13,500 Btu per pound.
- Lignite contains between 46 and 60 percent pure carbon and has a heat value of 5,500 to 8,300 Btu per pound.

Current and Potential Uses of Coal

Coal became a popular fuel in England in the nineteenth century because England sits on top of huge coal deposits. Coal was more plentiful than wood, which meant it was less expensive. The availability of coal along with inventions such as the steam engine allowed England to become the first truly industrialized nation.

Coal Is Increasingly Used to Generate Electricity

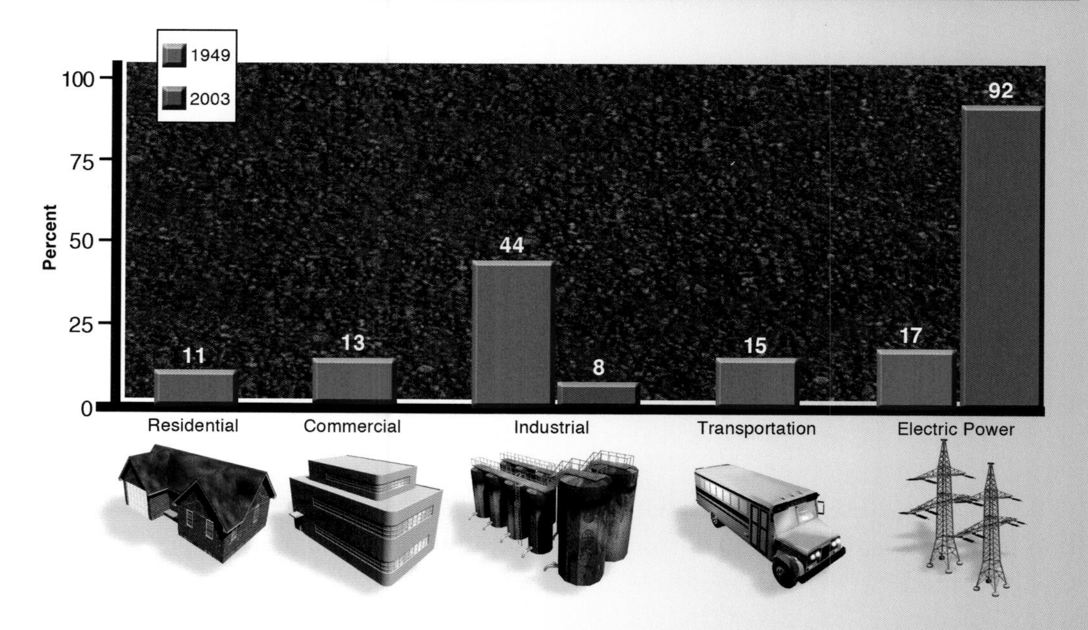

Source: U.S. Department of Energy, Energy Information Administration, Office of Energy Markets and End Use, *Annual Energy Review 2003*, September 7, 2004, http://www.eia.doe.gov/emeu/aer/pdf/aer.pdf.

During the nineteenth century and in the early part of the twentieth century, many people had coal-burning stoves in their homes. This system of heating had many drawbacks. It was messy, and people had to make sure they did not run out of coal. By the late twentieth century coal was no longer a common fuel for heating homes. As individual homeowners used less coal, industry used more.

Between 1940 and 1980 the amount of coal used by electrical power plants doubled every year. Coal also powers factories that make paper, iron, steel, ceramics, and cement. At the beginning of the twenty-first century over one-half of the electrical power plants in the United States were powered by coal.

Coal burns hotter and more efficiently than wood, and in many places it is more readily available. There is a great deal of coal in the world, so supplies are not likely to run out in the near future.

One of the drawbacks of using coal is that it has to be dug out. All methods of mining coal have problems associated with them. Coal is also very dirty. Coal dust coats anything it falls on, from buildings to people. Gases released by burning coal are big contributors to air pollution.

Environmental Impact of Coal

Coal is not environmentally friendly. It produces large amounts of pollution, which may contribute to acid rain and global warming. Mining it is often damaging to the environment, and transporting it is destructive as well. Most coal is moved around on trains, which are powered by pollution-causing diesel fuel.

Air Pollution. The difficulty with burning coal is that it rarely produces only carbon dioxide, water, and energy. If the temperature is not high enough or if not enough oxygen is available to keep the fire burning high, the coal is not completely burned. When that happens, the coal releases other substances into the air. These substances include:

- Carbon monoxide, which is toxic to humans and animals
- Soot, which is pure carbon dust and can turn buildings, trees, and animals black (The English invented glass-covered bookcases in the 1800s so their books would not get covered with soot.)
- Sulfur dioxide, sulfur trioxide, and nitrogen oxides, which become part of acid rain
- Lead, arsenic, barium, and other dangerous compounds that are in coal ash, which can float in the air or stay where the coal was burned and cause people to become ill

As mentioned, electrical power plants produce 67 percent of the United States sulfur dioxide emissions, 40 percent of carbon dioxide emissions, 25 percent of nitrogen oxide emissions, and 34 percent of mercury emissions. Coal-fired power plants account for over 95 percent of all these emissions.

New power plants may be less polluting than older ones, but most power plants operating in the United States as of 2005 still used older technology. Under the Clean Air Act older plants were prevented from expanding, in the hope that they would gradually close down and be replaced by modern facilities. The Clear Skies program enacted in 2003 by President George W. Bush removed this requirement, allowing older plants to keep operating and to expand their operations if they chose to do so.

Regardless of what developed countries of the twenty-first century do about emissions, China and other developing nations are using outdated technology that releases huge amounts of pollution. As the developing nations move towards resembling the developed world technologically, vast amounts of pollution travel around the world and end up in countries elsewhere.

Coal mining. Surface coal mining can leave huge holes in the

Power stations such as this one use steam from burning coal to generate electricity.

land and even destroy entire mountains. Water that flows over the mine site can flush pollutants into streams and rivers. Underground coal mining leaves behind tunnels in the ground, which can collapse suddenly. In the old days of mining, abandoned surface mines would turn into forbidding deserts, full of old rusted equipment.

Modern coal mining is very different, at least in the industrialized world. Due to several decades of pressure from consumers and environmental groups and new environmental laws, twenty-first century coal mining companies are much more careful about restoring the landscape after they take the coal from it. Miners save the topsoil and store local plants in greenhouses. Mining companies hire biologists, botanists (scientists who study plants), and fisheries experts to restore the environment as it was before mining began. Before laws required it, no mining company spent the money to avoid environmental harm.

Economic Impact of Coal

Coal started the industrial revolution in Europe in the late eighteenth century. Without coal, there would have been no factories, no steel, no trains, no steamships, and no electric lights. In the early twenty-first century coal is still a huge business. Coal mines bring in a great deal of money. In areas that have large coal deposits, most of the local population may be employed by the coal industry. The closing of a coal mine can harm a community by putting many townspeople out of work.

Societal Impact of Coal

Coal mining was one of the first industries to attract the attention of socially conscious lawmakers, who passed laws protecting workers. Coal mining was also one of the first industries in which workers organized, leading to the development of trade unions. Although mining techniques in the United States are much better than they were in the nineteenth century, coal miners still face more daily risks than most workers. Some health problems are much more common in coal miners than in other groups of people. Aside from the danger of being killed in

Scientists are searching for cleaner coal technologies so that burning coal will not contribute to air pollution and urban smog.

a mine collapse, coal miners are at risk of life-threatening lung diseases. People who live in coal mining regions depend on the coal industry for their income and do not want to see coal mining disappear. At the same time, they would like to see coal mining become safer and less destructive.

Issues, Challenges, and Obstacles in the Use of Coal

The demand for coal is expected to triple in the twenty-first century. Coal is the only fossil fuel that is likely to be in large supply in the year 2100, so people may become even more dependent on it. The U.S. Congress has encouraged coal producers to clean up coal technology since 1970. Scientists are trying to invent ways to use coal for fuel without causing pollution. These methods are called clean coal technologies and include the following:

- Coal gasification, by which coal is turned into gas that can be used for fuel, leaving the dangerous solid components in the mine
- Coal liquefaction, by which coal is turned into a petroleum-like liquid that can be used to power motor vehicles
- Coal pulverization, by which coal is broken into tiny particles before it is burned
- Use of hydrosizers, which are machines that use water to extract (take out or remove) the usable coal from mining waste to increase the amount of coal that can be retrieved from a mine
- Use of scrubbers and other devices to clean coal before, during, and after combustion to reduce the amount of pollution released into the atmosphere
- Use of bacteria to separate pollutants from organic components in coal so that the sulfur and other pollutants can be removed before burning
- Fluidized bed technology, which burns coal at a lower temperature or adds elements to the furnaces in coal plants to remove pollutants before they burn

Coal Gasification

Coal gasification is a process that converts coal to a gas that can be used as fuel. The main advantage of gasification is that it can remove pollutants from coal before the coal is burned, so the harmful substances are not released into the air. Coal gasification is a clean coal technology.

Coal gasification is done in stages. The first step is to crush

Converting Coal to Electricity

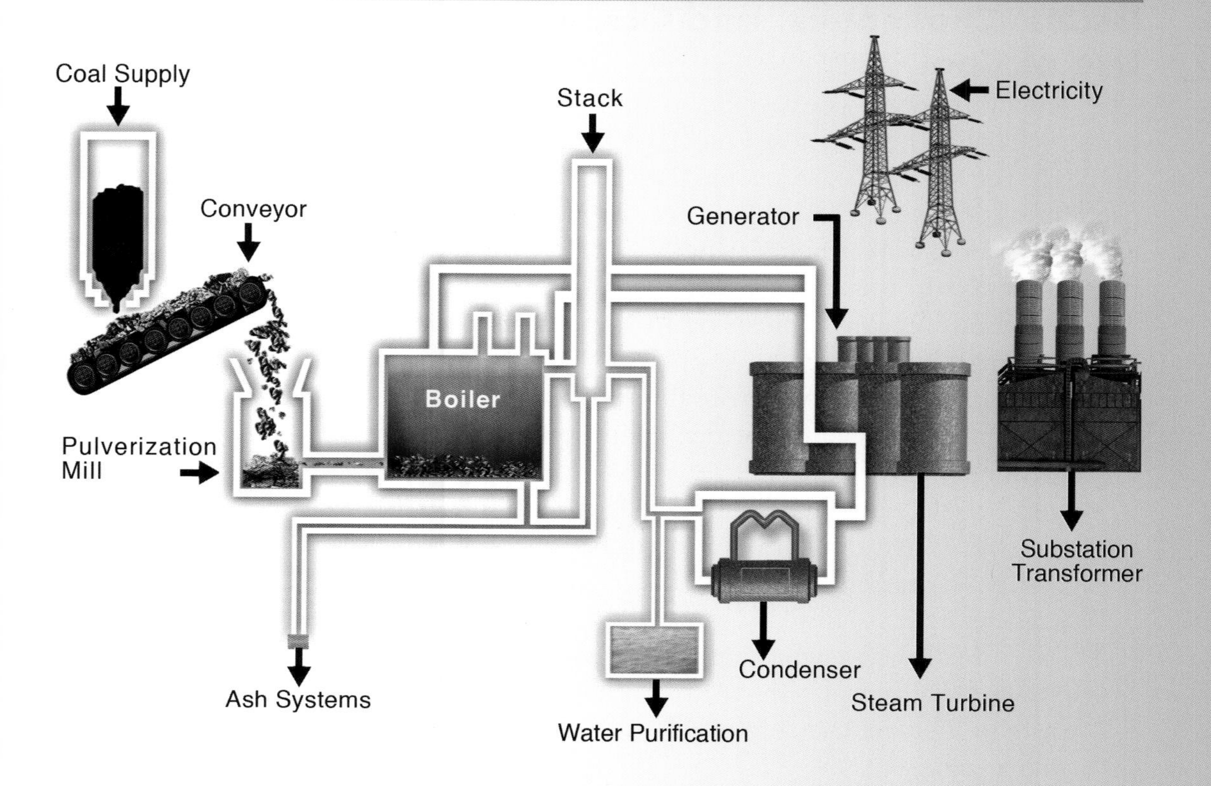

Source: World Coal Institute, *The Coal Resource*, May 2005.

and dry the coal. The crushed coal is placed in a boiler, where it is heated with air and steam. This heat causes chemical reactions that release a mix of gases that can then be used as fuel. The solid waste, or ash, remains in the boiler, where it can be collected and thrown away. Dangerous gases such as carbon dioxide and sulfur dioxide are removed in scrubbers like the ones in smokestacks at coal plants.

Gasification has been around for at least 100 years. The gas was widely piped and used as a fuel in Britain and many other European countries by 1900. Although it was used in other countries, in the United States it wasn't utilized during the first half of the century because petroleum and natural gas were inexpensive and plentiful. In the 1970s utility companies began considering gasification as a way to obey stricter environmental laws. Many people hope that coal gasification will be a valuable technology in the twenty-first century.

Current and Potential Uses of Coal Gasification

Coal gasification produces the following kinds of gases that can be used as fuel:

- Methane, which can be used as a substitute for natural gas
- Chemical synthesis gas consisting of carbon monoxide and hydrogen, which is used in the chemical industry to produce other chemicals, such as ammonia and methyl alcohol
- Medium-Btu gas, which is also made of carbon monoxide and hydrogen and used by utilities and industrial plants

Benefits and Drawbacks of Coal Gasification

Plants and factories that run on coal gasification technology have much lower emissions than traditional coal-burning plants, and their solid wastes are not hazardous. The waste products themselves can be useful. The sulfur dioxide scrubbers produce pure sulfur that can be used in other processes, and some scientists believe the ash can be used to build roads and buildings. Some people believe it may even be possible to use sewage or hazardous wastes to power the coal gasification boilers.

The greatest problem with coal gasification is cost. Using coal gasification technology to provide power to an industrial plant costs three times as much as using natural gas. Supporters of the technology hope that researchers will develop ways to make gasification less expensive. Coal gasification requires vast amounts of water, which creates a problem. For gasification to be cost-effective, the plants must be built near coal mines so that the coal does not have to travel far, and most coal mines in the United States are in western states, where water is limited and expensive.

On an environmental level, gasification has the potential to make coal a much less polluting fossil fuel. It will not have any impact on the environmental destruction caused by coal mining itself. However, coal mining is now much less destructive than it used to be.

Economically, coal gasification is much less efficient than burning coal directly; 30 to 40 percent of coal's energy is lost during the process of converting it to gas. Gasification would hardly be worth the cost of production if it were not for the environmental benefits it offers.

Scientists in Europe and the United States have been working to improve coal gasification techniques. They have been experimenting with using chemicals called catalysts to release the gases from coal. Using catalysts would allow gasification to occur at a lower temperature, which would make the process less expensive. Some scientists believe that the answer is to carry out gasification inside coal mines. Miners could pipe up the useful gases and leave the solid wastes underground. This idea is attractive because a large portion of coal reserves are nearly impossible to remove by the usual methods, and underground gasification would make those reserves available.

Eternal Coal Fires

Sometimes the coal inside a mine will catch on fire by accident. It can be nearly impossible to put out this kind of fire; drilling into the mine only adds oxygen to fuel the flames. A coal deposit in Tajikistan has supposedly been burning underground since 330 BCE when Alexander the Great visited the area. A network of coal mines in Centralia, Pennsylvania, caught fire in 1962 and is still burning. Someone had burned trash in an abandoned coal pit, and the coal vein ignited. The town had to be evacuated in the 1980s. Hundreds of coal mines are burning in the United States, but many more are burning in China and India, where mining development is proceeding too rapidly to control. In addition, coal mining produces tailings (coal mining wastes) that are put in large piles above ground; the tailings can also catch fire and burn for decades.

Does Burning Coal Threaten the Environment?

Burning coal releases tremendous amounts of energy, but the process can take a toll on the environment.

Mercury Emissions from Coal Plants Are a Serious Problem

Janet Larsen

In the following article Janet Larsen claims that coal plants are responsible for most mercury emissions. Mercury emitted by smokestacks falls back to earth and ends up in lakes, oceans, and rivers, where it is ingested by fish. People who eat tainted fish can experience serious health problems as a result, Larsen argues. For example, children can experience neurological and developmental problems as a result of exposure to mercury. Larsen is director of research at the Earth Policy Institute, an environmental watchdog organization.

Startling new research shows that one out of every six women of childbearing age in the United States may have blood mercury concentrations high enough to damage a developing fetus. This means that 630,000 of the 4 million babies born in the country each year are at risk of neurological damage because of exposure to dangerous mercury levels in the womb.

Fetuses, infants, and young children are most at risk for mercury damage to their nervous systems. New studies show that mercury exposure may also damage cardiovascular, immune, and reproductive systems. Chronic low-level exposure prenatally or in the early years of life can delay development and hamper performance in tests of attention, fine motor skills, language, visual spatial skills, and verbal memory. At high concen-

Janet Larsen, "Coal Takes Heavy Human Toll: Some 25,100 U.S. Deaths from Coal Use Largely Preventable," Earth Policy Institute, August 24, 2004.

trations, mercury can cause mental retardation, cerebral palsy, deafness, blindness, and even death.

Humans are exposed to mercury primarily by eating contaminated fish. Forty-five of the 50 states have issued consumption advisories limiting the eating of fish caught locally because of their high mercury content. New analyses of fish samples collected by the Environmental Protection Agency (EPA) from 500 lakes and reservoirs across the country found mercury in every single sample. In 55 percent of them, mercury levels exceeded the EPA's "safe" limit for a woman of average weight eating fish twice a week, and 76 percent exceeded limits for children under the age of three. Four out of five predator fish—those

States with the Most Mercury Emissions from Power Plants, 2002

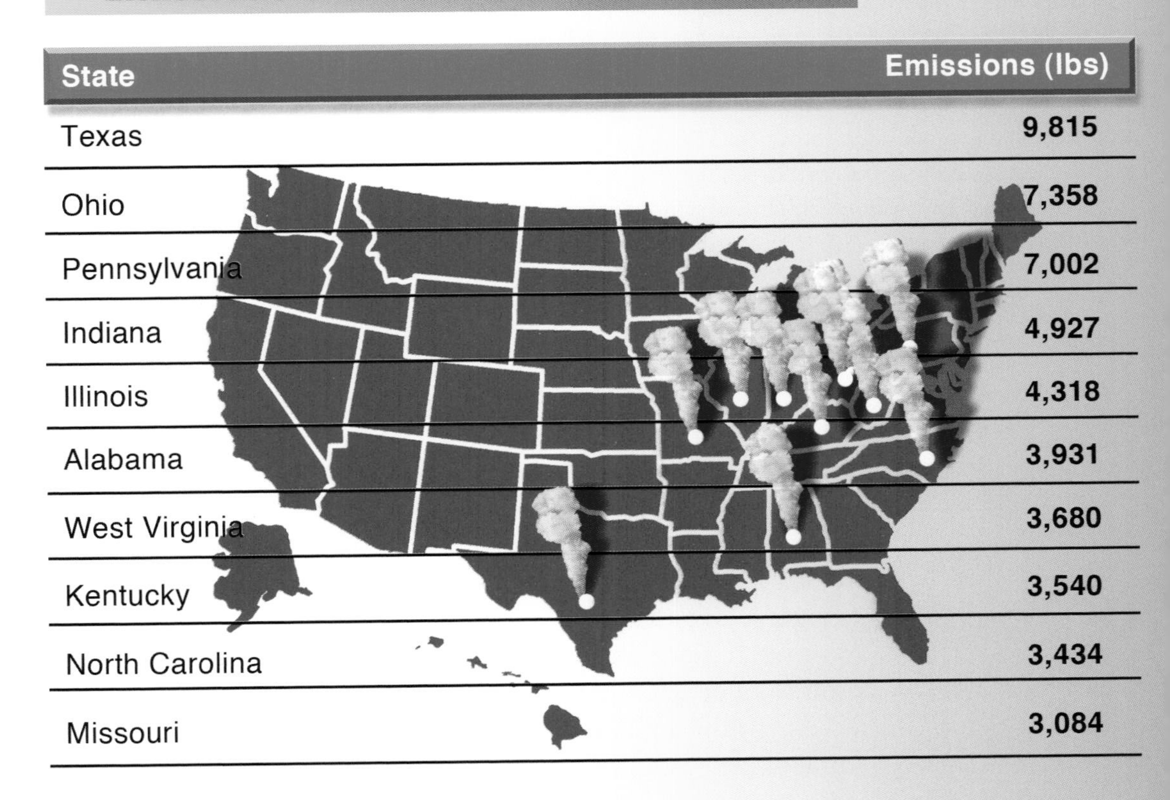

State	Emissions (lbs)
Texas	9,815
Ohio	7,358
Pennsylvania	7,002
Indiana	4,927
Illinois	4,318
Alabama	3,931
West Virginia	3,680
Kentucky	3,540
North Carolina	3,434
Missouri	3,084

Source: *U.S. EPA, 2002 Toxics Release Inventory*, www.epa.gov.

higher on the food chain, such as tuna or swordfish—exceeded the limits.

Coal Plants Are the Source

The largest source of mercury pollution is coal-fired power plants. Airborne mercury emitted by these facilities is deposited anywhere from within a few hundred kilometers of the smokestacks to across continents, far from its source. Biological processes change much of the deposited mercury into methylmercury, a potent neurotoxin that humans and other organisms readily absorb. Methylmercury easily travels up the aquatic food chain, accumulating at higher concentrations at each level. Larger predator species contain the most mercury, which is then passed on to those who eat them.

ANOTHER OPINION

American Babies Are at Risk

Scientists at the U.S. Environmental Protection Agency (EPA) estimate that one in six women of childbearing age in the U.S. has levels of mercury in her blood sufficiently high to put 630,000 of the four million babies born each year at risk of health problems due to mercury exposure.

U.S. Public Interest Research Group, *Fishing for Trouble: How Toxic Mercury Contaminates Fish in U.S. Waterways*, October 2004.

Since the industrial revolution began, mercury contamination in the environment has jumped threefold. The 600 plus coal-fired power plants in the United States, which produce over half of the country's electricity, burn 1 billion tons of coal and release 98,000 pounds (44 metric tons) of mercury into the air each year. Power plants yield an additional 81,000 pounds of mercury pollution in the form of solid waste, including fly ash and scrubber sludge, and 20,000 pounds of mercury from "cleaning" coal before it is burned. In sum, coal-fired power plants pollute the environment with some 200,000 pounds of mercury annually.

Solid wastes from coal-fired power plants also contain heavy metals like arsenic, selenium, chromium, and cadmium; carcinogenic organic compounds; and radioactive elements. These toxins can leach into streams and groundwater supplies, compromising people's health.

Other atmospheric emissions from burning coal include sulfur dioxide (SO_2), carbon dioxide (CO_2), particulate matter,

A sign near a fishing spot warns against consuming large amounts of mercury-laden fish. The links between mercury, fish, and health is an increasing topic of concern.

and nitrogen oxides (NO_x), which in turn form ground-level ozone. SO_2 and ozone are highly corrosive gases that cause respiratory distress and contribute to low birth weight and increased infant mortality. SO_2 and NO_x are also the primary causes of acid rain. CO_2 is the dominant gas responsible for the greenhouse effect that is warming the planet.

Particulate matter from coal combustion has long been known to harm the respiratory system. Now recent research has shown that small airborne particulate matter also can cross from the lungs into the bloodstream, leading to cardiac disease, heart attacks, strokes, and premature death.

In the United States, 23,600 deaths each year can be attributed to air pollution from power plants. Those dying prematurely due to exposure to particulate matter lose, on average, 14

Power Plants Emitting the Most Mercury Emissions, 2002

Facility	State	City	Air Emissions (lbs)
Limestone	TX	Jewett	1,800
TXU Monticello	TX	Mt. Pleasant	1,324
AEP Conesville	OH	Conesville	1,300
Reliant Keystone	PA	Shelocta	1,235
Jeffrey Energy Centre	KS	Saint Marys	1,216
W.A. Parish	TX	Thompsons	1,100
Alabama Power Miller	AL	Quinton	1,077
Martin Lake	TX	Tatum	1,027
AEP H.W. Pirkey Plant	TX	Hallsville	1,000
Georgia Power Scherer	GA	Juliette	943

Source: *U.S. EPA, 2002 Toxics Release Inventory*, www.epa.gov.

years of life. Burning coal also is responsible for some 554,000 asthma attacks, 16,200 cases of chronic bronchitis, and 38,200 non-fatal heart attacks each year. Atmospheric power plant pollution in the United States racks up an estimated annual health care bill of over $160 billion. . . .

Moving Beyond Coal

Using coal, a hazardous nineteenth-century fuel, when we have twenty-first-century alternatives is hard to understand. Renewable energy sources, such as wind and solar, do not require dangerous mining or mountaintop removal, nor do they pollute the air, land, and water with a slew of toxic chemicals. Full-cost pricing of coal to include the environmental damages and the enormous health care burden of using it, combined with removing antiquated subsidies on all fossil fuels, could go a long way toward encouraging more investment in renewables.

In addition, simple energy efficiency measures can reduce our reliance on fossil fuels and save money, too. Research from the Alliance to Save Energy indicates that improving efficiency standards for household appliances in the United States could allow 127 power plants to close. More stringent air conditioner efficiency standards could shut down 93 power plants. And raising the efficiency standards of both new and existing buildings through mechanisms like tax credits and energy codes could close 380 power plants. Using these methods to shut down the 600 most polluting coal-fired power plants in the country would be a boon for public health.

Several European countries have begun to lead the transition away from coal. In Germany, coal use has been cut in half since 1990, while expanding wind electric generation is taking its place. Coal use in the United Kingdom has dropped by 46 percent over the same period, offset by efficiency gains and a shift toward natural gas. Plans are moving ahead for a huge expansion in wind energy in the U.K. and other European countries.

By moving beyond coal, the United States could avoid a legacy of smog-filled skies, acid rain, polluted waterways, contaminated fish, and scarred landscapes. This could each year save some 25,000 lives, reduce respiratory and cardiovascular illnesses, avert potential neurological damage for 630,000 babies, and erase a health care bill of over $160 billion.

Mercury Emissions from Coal Plants Are Not a Serious Problem

Robert Peltier

Robert Peltier is the editor in chief of *Power* magazine, an electric energy trade journal. In the following article Peltier argues that the government is wrongheaded in passing tighter controls on mercury emissions from coal power plants. According to Peltier, there is no solid evidence to justify fears that mercury—a naturally occurring element—is dangerous to humans. But even if it were worthwhile to reduce mercury emissions, Peltier maintains, U.S. power plants are the wrong target. The primary contributor of global coal pollution is China.

Few would deny the success of the cap-and-trade program[1] to reduce acid rain as well as the many NO_x [nitrogen oxides], SO_x [sulfur oxides], and particulate reduction projects that have made America's air much cleaner since the 1970 Clean Air Act. The rules that spawned those projects were based on strong science and enjoyed strong public support. Unfortunately, the same can't be said for the mercury regulations . . . issued [in] March [2005 by the Environmental Protection Agency (EPA)]. In their case, a thin veneer of science covers a rotten core of politics.

1. A cap-and-trade program places a limit (cap) on the amount of pollution emitted from all regulated sources (such as power plants), but individual sources can trade their emission allowances (if their emissions fall under their allotted share) to other sources that exceed the limits.

Robert Peltier, "Mercury Mockery," *Power*, vol. 148, October 2004, pp. 1–4. Reproduced by permission.

False Claims Lead to Poor Legislation

The effort to regulate mercury began after the Natural Resources Defense Council sued the EPA to do something about the pollutant in 1994. But Carol Browner, then head of the EPA, ignored the suit until the day after Al Gore conceded the [U.S. presidential] election in 2000. The problem was then thrown to the Bush administration to deal with. Now Browner is wailing over the president's "Clear Skies" proposal to reduce mercury emissions from power plants by 70% by 2018. This marks the first time the EPA has made a case to regulate a hazardous air pollutant from coal- and oil-fired generators.

The political debate has spilled over into the mainstream media with claims that mercury-contaminated fish are poisoning children and putting pregnant women at risk. Most

The diet of Faroe Islands residents consists mainly of mercury-contaminated whale, yet no serious health affects have been observed among its population.

disturbing is the lack of credible scientific evidence to make the causal link between mercury emissions from power plants, mercury in fish (especially tuna), and the health effects of eating those fish.

Although U.S. mercury emissions have fallen 42% over the past decade, a Princeton University study found no change in mercury levels in Pacific tuna since 1970. Even if the world got rid of every power plant, fish still would ingest mercury, because 55% of the world's emissions of the element come from nature. Studies of 550-year-old Aleutian mummies show they contained more mercury than do people today. As one pundit put it, "It's a whole lot abalone."

Conflicting Evidence About Mercury's Health Effects

One scientific study often cited by ardent environmentalists examined Faroe Island children [the Faroe Islands lie between Scotland and Iceland]. Faroe islanders' diet consists mainly of seafood (including whale) loaded with mercury. Seventeen neuropsychological tests of their children showed that some scored slightly below average on just three of the tests. The researchers failed to demonstrate a statistical correlation between mercury consumption (or even the consumption of other toxins such as PCBs [polluting organic compounds found in paints, pesticides, oils, etc.] and DDT [an insecticide]) and "brain damage."

The EPA's proposed "safe" levels of mercury are, unfortunately, based on the Faroe Island study; they are set at one-tenth the smallest amount of mercury connected with a lower Faroe test score. The U.S. Food and Drug Administration has noted that women with over the U.S. limit have an eightfold margin of safety based on the Faroe study.

ANOTHER OPINION

There Is No Link Between the Mercury in Humans and That Produced by Power Plants

In the case of power plants, we don't even know how much [mercury] gets taken up by humans. That's because no one has ever bothered to see if the mercury in Americans largely resembles the mercury, in its chemical signature, that comes out of power plants.

Patrick J. Michaels, Cato Institute, March 19, 2003, www.cato.org.

On the other hand, consider a University of Rochester study that followed a group of Seychelles Island children from birth until the age of nine. [The Seychelles are an island nation in the Indian Ocean.] Their mothers ate similar fish as frequently as American women do—but the mercury content of the island women's fish was 10 times higher, and the women had an average of six times as much mercury in their bodies. Yet researchers found their children to be healthy. This study was discounted by regulators.

The U.S. Is Not to Blame for Mercury Emissions

Let's put mercury emissions from U.S. sources into perspective. The U.S. House Committee on Resources estimates that only 1% of total worldwide emissions of mercury come from U.S. utilities. Not surprisingly, coal-crazy China is responsible for more than half of the world's emissions of the pollutant: 495 tons annually, a figure that is expected to increase by more than 40 tons over the next two to five years [by 2009].

An EPRI [Electric Power Research Institute] study also notes that much of the mercury in the U.S. ecosystem appears to originate in Asia and is carried across the Pacific by prevailing winds. Recent studies used aircraft outfitted to make direct measurements to track mercury plumes from China's industrial southeast across the Pacific and into western states.

In my opinion, it is now too late to hope that any rational thought will inform the process of balancing the costs of controlling power plant mercury emissions against their supposed negative health impacts. Federal mercury regulations . . . finally hit the street [in 2005]. Whether or not they make sense, we in the U.S. power generation industry will have to learn to live with them.

The Coal Industry Is Destroying the Environment

Jennifer Hattam

Jennifer Hattam is the associate editor of *Sierra*, an environmental magazine. In the following article Hattam discusses grassroots efforts in West Virginia to fight the coal industry's practices. According to local activists, coal mining operations known as mountaintop removal destroy mountain forests and carve deep ruts into hillsides. The debris from mountaintop removal is then carelessly dumped over the mountainsides to litter the ground and waterways below. In addition, Hattam writes, toxic byproducts of mining operations are released into the environment, poisoning wildlife and people. Although activists are beginning to protest these reckless practices, Hattam argues that the nation's demand for coal has given mine owners the power and influence to continue their destructive ways unchecked.

Deep in the Coal River Valley of West Virginia, the town of Whitesville clings to life along State Route 3. Its three-block downtown is marked by empty lots, boarded-up windows, and two funeral homes, and there's scarcely a person to be seen. The outskirts seem cheerier, with laughter bouncing out of the swimming pool and across the baseball field. But in a state wracked by turmoil since it was torn out of Virginia during the Civil War, even the bright spots are haunted by their past. . . .

Jennifer Hattam, "Dethroning King Coal," *Sierra*, vol. 88, pp. 1–8.

Mountaintop Removal

Coal built Whitesville, and other towns like it throughout Appalachia, but now coal is ripping the region apart. "My people have had to live with oppression for over 130 years," says Julia Bonds, 51, whose family includes three generations of coal miners. "But this new type of mining is more aggressive than ever. The coal industry is destroying our culture and our environment."

The new type of mining, aptly called "mountaintop removal," has claimed nearly a fifth of southwestern West Virginia's peaks. Before the early 1960s, getting coal out of the ground meant sending men down into it. Then companies found that they could get at more coal, for less money, by simply tearing off the earth on top. Surface (or "strip") mining accelerated after the oil crises of the 1970s increased demand for domestic fuels, and

In "mountaintop removal" or strip-mining, mountains are destroyed by blasting their tops off to expose coal.

again in the 1980s as earthmoving machines grew bigger and more powerful. With the latest removal techniques, hundreds of feet of dirt, plants, and rock above the coal seam are blasted off and dumped over the side of the mountain. This "overburden" smothers streams and pollutes the air, and the resulting erosion has led to some of the worst flooding in state history.

In May [2003], a study by five government agencies calculated the toll mountaintop removal has taken in the Appalachian coalfields: 724 miles of streams buried and over 300,000 acres of forests obliterated. The deforestation is expected to double over the next decade. But instead of tougher regulations, the Bush administration proposed to "streamline" the review of new mining permits. It has also revised the Clean Water Act to legalize the already common practice of dumping mountain remnants into waterways as "fill." A local bumper sticker sums up events pretty well: "I have been to the mountaintop, but it wasn't there."

Fighting Coal's Ruinous Reign

Julia Bonds is fighting to end coal's ruinous reign. A former Pizza Hut waitress and convenience-store clerk, for the past five years [since 1998] Bonds has been the community outreach coordinator for a tiny grassroots organization, Coal River Mountain Watch. Scarcely five feet tall, with dark hair, soft features, and a preference for baggy T-shirts, leggings, and sneakers, Bonds doesn't seem very intimidating. Until she opens her mouth. "We are living with domestic terrorism from these coal barons," she told me 15 minutes into our first meeting. "And our lapdog politicians are working hand in hand with the corporations that put them in place to destroy our children's world. They think we're a bunch of ignorant hillbillies, but you don't have to be very smart to figure that one out, do you?"

Bonds spends much of her time meeting with beleaguered residents, helping them navigate the maze of permitting laws and regulatory agencies that govern mining operations. (Or, as she puts it, "educatin', motivatin', and communicatin'.") One of only three staffers at Coal River Mountain Watch, she also organizes protests, lobbies at the state capitol, and answers the constantly ringing phone. Since April [2003], when her efforts

Source: West Virginia Geological and Economic Survey, October 1998.

to stop mountaintop removal won her a Goldman Environmental Prize for grassroots activism, people have been calling from around the country, and even the world, seeking advice on how to keep mining from devastating their communities. When I visited, she hadn't had a day off in three weeks. "We're spread too thin here," she sighs.

Bonds's ancestors settled in Marfork Hollow (or "holler," as the locals say) after the Revolutionary War. . . . She looks back on her Marfork childhood fondly, and raised her own daughter there. Then, in 1993, the A.T. Massey Coal Company moved in and began blasting. After a while, coal dust permeated Bonds's home, and her young grandson, Andrew, developed asthma. "I started to notice black-water spills in the stream that six generations of my family had enjoyed," Bonds says. "One day Andrew stood in that stream, and the fish were dead all around his feet. I knew something was very, very wrong, so I began to open my eyes and pay attention."

When she investigated, she learned that Massey, a major operator throughout the Coal River Valley, was building a large slurry dam at the head of her hollow. There are 136 such dams, or "impoundments," in the state. Together they hold billions of gallons of wastewater, rock, and mining's toxic byproducts, including mercury, lead, arsenic, and chromium. With accidental discharges a real danger—a 300-million-gallon spill by a Massey subsidiary in Kentucky recently created a state of emergency for ten counties—the people living below these dams sleep uneasily. Nervous neighbors began moving away. Bonds held out for years, but when her grandson, then 8, started concocting evacuation plans, she knew it was time to go.

Bonds's new home [is] on a grassy, open hill some ten miles away from Marfork. . . .

Devastated Mountain Environments

To really understand what it's like to live with mountaintop removal, Bonds insists, I've got to meet people like Joe and Judith Barnett, longtime residents of Clearfork Hollow. "We used to go up into the hills, camping, picking ginseng, all the things that us country people do," says Joe, who worked as a miner for 26 years but is now a vocal critic of the industry. "Now it's all gone." What they have in its place are photo albums full of dismal pictures: of clearcutting and explosions right behind their home; of tree debris washing into the creeks and coal trucks carving up their backyard; of cracks in their house from three years of blasting.

The 15-mile drive to Clearfork Hollow is winding and mostly scenic, except for a few piles of unusable coal along the roadside. As we turn off the main route, the hills close in around the car, wrapping us in green. Then a break in the trees reveals a deep gouge on the mountainside, a dirty, barren slope riddled with electric-blue puddles. When we get out of the car, a nearby resident comes over to talk to Bonds. Looking up at the denuded hillside and shaking her head, the young woman says, "If my daddy could see what they'd done to those mountains, he'd cry.". . .

Hiding the Damages

The very land that inspires West Virginians to stand up for their home makes it difficult to organize: "Nothing's close to anything," Bonds says. "You have to drive around the mountains to get from one place to another." It also makes it easy for coal companies to hide their damages. When you fly in on a rattling 30-seat prop plane, the scars of mining and logging are all too clear. The remaining peaks appear tightly clustered; Bonds compares it to "a sleeping dragon, all coiled up on itself." On

An open pit near a residential area in West Virginia contains mining wastes, including water polluted with sulphuric acid from the strip mining process.

the ground, you can find your way through the narrow valleys, but the devastation is usually hidden behind the next ridge. You might catch a whiff of diesel on a placid hillside, or hear what sounds like a distant freeway (actually the rush of natural gas being let off) when there are no roads in sight. But with the coal companies controlling most of the land, even longtime residents rarely see the gouged mountains and sludge dams that threaten their future.

For all the trouble coal has brought, its hold on the community is still strong. Mining coal and burning it in power plants creates almost two-thirds of the business-tax revenue in the state, one of the poorest in the country. . . . Coal permeates West Virginia politics, with hefty campaign contributions to

Source: Adapted from Figure 7.6. "Coal Mining Productivity: Total, 1949–2003," in *Annual Energy Review 2003*, U.S. Department of Energy, Energy Information Administration, Office of Energy Markets and End Use, September 7, 2004, http://www.eia.doe.gov/emeu/aer/pdf/aer.pdf.

state lawmakers and donations to local schools. Whitesville's mayor works for Massey, and a huge billboard on the road into town asks, "Coal supports our schools. Do you support Coal?" Many people still do, whether out of a sense of indebtedness for the prosperity coal brought in the past, or fear for their survival in the present. Highly mechanized mountaintop removal cut mining jobs by nearly half in the last decade and sapped labor's strength. The mostly nonunion miners are scared, says Joe Barnett. "They won't allow their wives to speak out. They get mad at me for speaking out.". . .

Gathering Evidence of Wrongdoing

Two people who aren't frightened are Mary Miller and Pauline Canterberry, fiery septuagenarians known as the "Sylvester Dustbusters." Since Massey subsidiary Elk Run Coal Company opened a preparation plant just down the road in 1998, over the firm opposition of residents, their town of Sylvester has been blanketed with coal dust. "You can't hang out clothes, you can't even open the windows," Miller says. "If you want to sit on your porch, you have to wipe off the dust every day." The local elementary school is being closed, and many residents have left, but with Bonds's inspiration and guidance, Miller and Canterberry are fighting to save their town, because they just can't see living anywhere else.

Finishing each other's sentences and laughing at inside jokes, Miller and Canterberry explain their five-year battle. How they've collected boxes upon boxes of carefully labeled Ziploc bags, each containing a paper towel covered in coal dust that they wiped from neighbors' houses. How they've complained to state regulators with little result. How Miller's house, appraised at $144,000, is now worth only $12,000 on account of the dust. ("That's not even going to bury me!" she exclaims.) How they've organized their neighbors to sign petitions, demand hearings, and join a lawsuit against Elk Run. How the community has won jury awards and cleanup orders, but the company ties them up in appeals. "They think they're either going to kill us or that we're going to give up and quit," Miller says. "But I got news for them.". . .

A stream in West Virginia runs brown from mining waste and pollutants such as sulphuric acid and iron pyrites.

Alternatives to Rapacious Mining

While coal use dropped 30 percent over the last 15 years in western Europe, the United States is burning more coal than ever: Half the nation's electricity comes from coal-fired plants. They also churn out massive amounts of mercury, greenhouse gases, and more smog-causing nitrogen oxide emissions than all the nation's cars, vans, and SUVs combined. By some estimates, these pollutants cause almost 30,000 deaths each year, extending the risks of coal mining far beyond the coalfields.

For many environmentalists these problems have an obvious solution: Stop mining and burning coal. For West Virginia activists like Bonds, it's not so simple. Her no-nonsense manner and family ties to the coal industry have helped her work successfully with the United Mine Workers of America [UMWA] on issues like Massey's environmental and safety record and the mammoth coal trucks that regularly run overloaded on the valley's narrow, winding roads. But the UMWA won't take a stand against mountaintop removal. Many residents share the same reluctance.

So Bonds must walk a fine line between supporting "responsible" mining now, and preparing for a future without it. . . . She lobbies elected officials to increase economic diversity in the state—to bring in jobs in alternative energy, or to help traditional pastimes like collecting medicinal herbs, quilting, and wood carving to grow into sustainable businesses. Tourism, which is adding more to state coffers each year while coal revenues decline, could provide another solution. But these possibilities depend on keeping the environment and the culture intact now.

"Our state has long been pillaged and raped for its natural resources, and at first, that was acceptable, because it provided our livelihood," says Bonds. But with the loss of jobs, "a veil has been lifted and people can actually see what's happening." While driving into downtown Charleston for a protest, she smiles as she points out graffiti scrawled on a wall: The air is full of the dreams of sleeping people. Her people may still be slumbering, she says, but they're starting to stir.

CHAPTER 3

Is Coal the Energy of the Future?

Because coal is one of the earth's only abundant fossil fuels, it is likely to play some role in future energy plans.

The Pros and Cons of Investing in Clean Coal Technologies

Katie Benner

In the following article Katie Benner, a staff writer for *CNN Money* online magazine, discusses the debate over America's adoption of clean coal technologies. Clean coal technologies are those that remove or limit the amount of harmful pollutants—such as mercury emissions and carbon dioxide (CO_2)—that are generated when coal is burned. According to Benner, environmentalists are advocating that America's coal plants utilize carbon sequestration to trap CO_2 before it is released into the air. Critics, however, argue that such processes are too expensive and have not been proven to work. Still others in the debate contend that investing in alternatives to coal energy may bring better results than embracing costly and unproven coal technologies.

Big money is pouring into "clean coal"—hyped as an environmentally friendly resource that can keep the lights on and break our dependence on foreign oil—but some critics question whether the investment is worth it.

The Bush administration currently spends about $400 million a year on coal research, not much compared with the $1.3 billion spent annually on renewable resources, such as solar and wind power, according to the federal Energy Information Administration (EIA).

But the administration has proposed another $2 billion for its

Katie Benner, "Clean Coal: A Good Investment?" *CNN/Money*, October 19, 2004, pp. 1–4. Reproduced by permission. http://money.cnn.com.

clean coal program, on top of $2 billion in subsidies for the coal sector. Meanwhile, Sen. John Kerry has pledged to spend $10 billion on clean coal technology, including $2 billion to demonstrate the commercial viability of clean coal.

In an election year when votes in coal producing swing states like Pennsylvania and West Virginia are crucial, these promises come as little surprise. And few disagree that the nation needs alternate, more efficient sources of energy. But critics say that newer "clean coal" technology, for all its promised benefits, is expensive. And some say that the technology, despite its positive-sounding name, will create expensive environmental headaches.

The Need for Power

"With nuclear and hydro resources pretty much tapped out, it comes down to a debate between coal and gas," said Mark Morey, director of the Cambridge Energy Resource Association's North America power group.

According to the EIA, coal is plentiful and cheap, with domestic supplies projected to last two centuries or more. About half the nation's electricity is already generated by coal-fired plants, so there's an infrastructure for coal in place.

And with electricity demand expected to grow sharply in coming decades, proponents say clean coal is the way to go. "Clean coal technology is the future," said Ohio Coal Association President Mike Carey.

Some big companies are betting heavily on the technology. General Electric (Research) and Bechtel are jointly developing a model for coal gasification plants, which convert coal into a gas. The plants are considered the most vaunted of the clean coal technologies by the EIA and coal industry leaders.

An Expensive Proposal

Clean coal plants aren't cheap to build, and costs to dispose of their waste are steep.

Bechtel said the initial cost to build a coal gasification plant is 25 percent more than a medium-sized conventional coal-fired power plant. A conventional plant costs about $780 million to

There is concern that the increased use of coal-fired power plants will contribute to harmful emissions, such as carbon dioxide and other greenhouse gases.

build, according to Bechtel, so a comparable coal-gas plant would cost about $975 million.

"There are a lot of parallels between coal and nuclear energy," said Cambridge Energy's Morey. "The plants are really expensive to build and there's an issue about disposing of large amounts of [carbon dioxide] waste that could get really costly."

While there has never been a law regulating carbon dioxide emissions in the U.S., many scientists, utility analysts, environmentalists and business executives admit that CO_2 emissions are the chief cause of global warming.

"In ways we've looked at pollution in the past, coal has cleaned up. But the bigger problem we face now is carbon dioxide, which clean coal plants still emit," said Dave Hamilton, the Sierra Club's director of Global Warming and Energy Programs.

World Carbon Dioxide Emissions from Coal Use by Region
(Million Metric Tons Carbon Dioxide)

Region / Country	History			Projections				Average Annual Percent Change, 2002-2025
	1990	2001	2002	2010	2015	2020	2025	
Mature Market Economies								
United States	1,784	2,042	2,070	2,335	2,407	2,561	2,858	1.4
Canada	123	148	154	166	169	172	210	1.4
Mexico	15	24	23	36	39	41	42	2.6
Western Europe	1,160	849	825	783	740	699	661	-1.0
Japan	245	364	375	386	380	376	372	0.0
Australia/New Zealand	138	229	247	289	291	314	317	1.1
Transitional Economies								
Former Soviet Union	1,222	667	671	761	781	796	812	0.8
Eastern Europe	685	409	397	408	412	414	419	0.2
Emerging Economies								
China	1,886	2,472	2,582	4,181	4,911	5,514	5,887	3.6
India	394	684	698	903	1,019	1,119	1,222	2.5
South Korea	90	152	161	196	235	263	286	2.5
Other Asia	237	371	389	504	559	592	629	2.1
Middle East	72	110	100	138	140	140	139	1.4
Africa	271	340	338	421	453	485	486	1.6
Brazil	34	40	41	54	59	66	74	2.6
Other Central/South America	20	26	32	44	47	48	46	1.6
Total World	8,375	8,928	9,105	11,604	12,642	13,600	14,458	2.0

Source: Energy Information Administration (EIA), *International Energy Annual 2002*, www.eia.gov.

"Businesses know carbon dioxide will be regulated in the future and would rather make it part of the cost to build a new plant now rather than wait and have to add technology," said Morey. "These plants are 40- to 50-year investments."

"Many ways of taking care of carbon dioxide are being studied, particularly carbon sequestration," said Carey. Trapping and holding CO_2 is the most popular method of dealing with emissions from coal-gas plants; and it's part of President Bush's FutureGen initiative to create the world's first zero-emissions fossil fuel plant.

But trapping carbon is expensive. For an average traditional coal-fired plant, which produces some 750 million tons of carbon a year, the annual cost of trapping CO_2 is about $31 million a year, said Stephan Singer, head of European Climate and Energy policy with WWF International, which works closely with the EU on climate change and energy.

Analysts and environmentalists also say there's little evidence to show this process will ever work.

"If it all leaks, then you're right back where you started, plus you've wasted all that money," said Hamilton.

If Not Coal . . .

Environmentalists aren't the only ones questioning whether clean coal is worth it.

Dave Schanzer, a utilities analyst with Janney Montgomery Scott, said billions should not be spent on making the country more dependent on coal.

"The answer is nuclear power," Schanzer said. "Spent nuclear fuel has to be stored safely, but we have that technology now." In contrast, he added, "You have to store CO_2, and we don't even know if it can be done. Using the technology we've got can prevent polluting the environment and the massive clean-up."

While Schanzer may take a minority view in the U.S. on nuclear power, the Sierra Club's Hamilton agreed money should be invested in improving existing technology before spending billions on new technologies.

And with coal now providing 50 percent of the nation's power, Schanzer added, "Every systems operator will tell you a balanced fuel mix is the best way to provide electricity. We should be using more of what we have and making it more efficient."

"Attacking energy waste is the cheapest and cleanest thing we can do to address the energy crisis," added Hamilton. "We have no ethical problem with making dirty things cleaner, but by simply investing in energy efficiently we could create 1.4 million jobs by 2025 and reduce the overall electricity load by 10 percent."

Comparing Coal with Other Energy Sources

Margaret Kriz

In the following selection Margaret Kriz compares the costs and benefits of various energy sources including coal, natural gas, nuclear power, and renewables such as wind power. Although the burning of coal produces pollution, she asserts that coal will remain the nation's dominant energy source. Natural gas is too expensive, nuclear power produces dangerous toxic waste, and renewable energy sources are simply too inefficient, Kriz maintains. Kriz is a correspondent who covers environmental and energy issues for the *National Journal*.

Modern American society perches atop a mountain of coal-fired power plants. Since the late 1940s, 1,622 of them have been brought on line, and most are still in operation. King Coal provides half of the nation's electricity. Nuclear power supplies just one-fifth, and another fifth comes from natural gas. Oil and renewable resources—mostly hydropower—supply the remainder.

Coal and pollution have always gone hand in hand. But beginning in the early 1970s, Congress mandated a cleanup of the nation's air by passing a series of increasingly tough air-pollution control laws—led by the landmark Clean Air Act—aimed at forcing corporate America to limit the chemicals it was sending

Margaret Kriz, "King Coal's Resurgence," *National Journal*, vol. 36, June 26, 2004, pp. 1–9.

up smokestacks. The laws took special aim at coal-fired power plants. To comply, most of those facilities installed "scrubbers" and other expensive pollution control equipment. Yet coal-burning generators continue to be a major cause of smog, acid rain, water pollution, and global warming.

Coal's Dark Side

According to the Environmental Protection Agency [EPA], in 2002, the electricity industry emitted 63 percent of the nation's sulfur dioxide pollution, 39 percent of the man-made carbon dioxide, 33 percent of the mercury, and 22 percent of the nitrogen oxides. The vast majority of that pollution comes from coal-fired plants.

Coal provides about half of America's power because it is a cheap, abundant energy source.

And the nation's dirty air is affecting Americans' health. A new study, released on June 9 [2004] and based on EPA data, indicates that air pollution from coal-fired power plants causes 24,000 premature deaths a year, including 2,800 from lung cancer, and leads to 38,200 nonlethal heart attacks. . . .

Little wonder, then, that environmental groups are horrified at coal's resurging popularity among utility CEOs. Environmentalists argue that even though the new power plants would be a breed apart from the smoke-belching dinosaurs of the past, they would do more harm than would other types of power plants.

Critics are particularly worried that additional coal-fired plants will increase emissions of the greenhouse gas carbon dioxide. States in the Northeast and on the West Coast are considering limits on carbon dioxide emissions. And industry executives expect that federal regulations will eventually be imposed on CO_2. In hopes of delaying that eventuality, business groups have thrown their support behind the Bush administration's proposal for voluntary reductions in CO_2 pollution. Already, the coal industry is benefiting from the Bush administration's postponement of some pollution-control deadlines and from its easing of requirements that existing coal-fired plants install new pollution controls when expanding. . . .

The Need for More Energy

While coal's friends and foes spar over environmental issues, advocates of other fuel sources are eagerly watching. Nuclear energy's champions say their technology is the answer to air-pollution problems, because nuclear power plants produce no carbon dioxide. The nation's 103 operating nuclear plants do, however, produce tons of radioactive waste that does not yet have a permanent home. No new nuclear power plants have been ordered in the United States since the partial meltdown of Pennsylvania's Three Mile Island plant in 1979. But nuclear power officials say their industry is poised for a renaissance. At most, however, only a handful of nuclear plants will be built over the next 20 years.

The use of renewable energy sources, particularly wind power, has steadily expanded over the past decade. That growth

While nuclear power plants such as this one do not emit carbon dioxide, they produce dangerous radioactive waste and could be targeted by terrorists.

was fueled by a federal investment tax credit, which gave utilities 1.8 cents for every kilowatt hour of power generated from wind. Adopted in 1995, the tax credit expired in 2003.[1]

Wind could never match the growing demand for electricity, however. Under the most optimistic scenario advanced by industry executives, wind power might produce 6 percent of the nation's electricity by 2020—up from less than one-half of 1 percent today. . . .

By 2010, according to the Energy Department's Energy Information Administration, the nation will need to substantially increase the construction of power plants to keep up with electricity demand. When that happens, power companies will choose

1. It was renewed in 2005.

coal. And Lawrence Makovich, senior director of Cambridge Energy Research Associates' Americas division, warns that environmental mandates could then cause electricity prices to surge.

"I'm raising an alarm here," said Makovich, who forecasts that natural gas prices will remain high. "Over the next decade or so, we're in a jam. We are a very energy-intensive world, and we have to set realistic options to keep that in place. . . . You can get cleaner coal-fired generation, but it costs you something."

Economics Win Out

For the time being, however, the market appears to be discounting the prospect of tougher environmental controls on coal, said Steve Piper, managing director of power forecasting at Platts, an energy-research company. "If you weigh the current economics of electricity generation against a potential, speculative carbon levy in the future, today's economics are winning out," and investors are backing coal, he said.

Jack Gerard, president of the National Mining Association, the trade group representing coal-mining companies, says the nation is on the brink of a coal boom. "The pendulum is swinging back toward more of a balance," he said. "The volatility of natural gas prices is such that we need to seriously look at coal-fired power."

Coal plants have significant drawbacks—aside from producing air pollution. Coal-fired facilities are more expensive to construct than gas-powered ones, take longer to build, and are more difficult to site because they are larger and more harmful to the environment. But coal offers one colossal benefit: The United States has plenty of it. According to the U.S. Geological Survey, this country has enough coal to power it for 230 years at the current rate of use. By comparison, the United States has just a 60-year supply of natural gas, according to the Colorado School of Mines.

That's why so many electricity companies, anxious to avoid high natural gas prices, are taking a hard look at building coal plants. . . .

During the 1990s, natural gas power plants were in vogue because "gas was much cheaper [than today], it takes far less time

A liquefied natural gas (LNG) tank dwarfs the tugboat towing it. It remains to be seen whether LNG represents the future of energy.

to build a gas plant, and it's easier to get permitted," noted Lynne H. Church, president of the Electric Power Supply Association, which represents the independent electric companies that built most of those gas plants. "From an environmental standpoint, it's less polluting," she added. "And you need less land mass to site a plant," because gas facilities are smaller and don't need to have railroad cars full of coal nearby.

But the gas-versus-coal calculus shifted as gas prices more than tripled—from $2 per million British thermal units of electricity in 2001 to more than $6.50 as of early June [2004]. And prices could get much higher this summer as Americans crank up their air conditioners, according to a June 8 [2004] report by the National Gas Supply Association.

Analysts disagree on how climbing prices will affect the long-term prospects of natural gas as a source of electricity. Some argue that the high costs will slash orders for new gas-fired plants. . . .

Yet the Energy Information Administration's annual energy outlook report, released in February [2004], predicted that 60 percent of the power capacity built over the next 20 years would use natural gas. And Roger Cooper, the American Gas Association's executive vice president for policy analysis, notes that new coal plants aren't likely to be welcome in parts of the

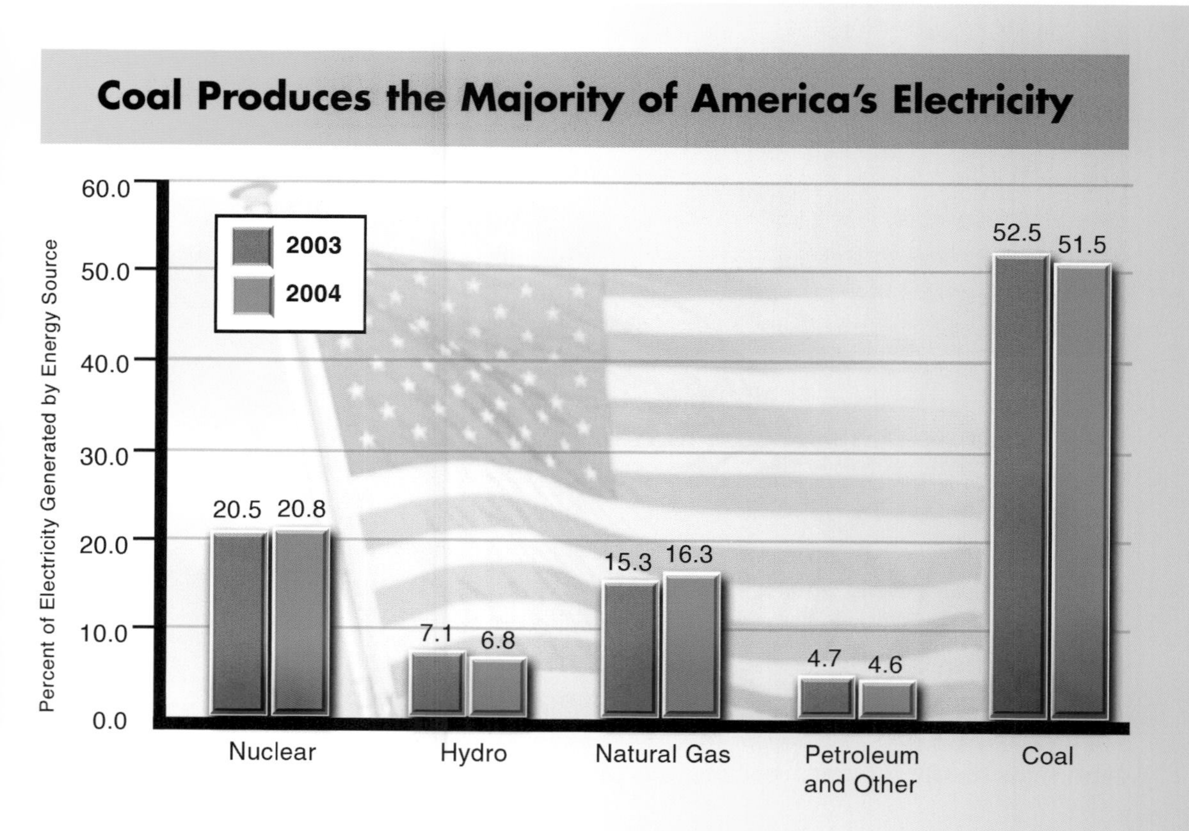

Source: U.S. Energy Information Administration, April 20, 2005, www.eia.doe.gov.

country where the air already fails to meet EPA standards. Environmental concerns might lead power companies to stick with natural gas, he said. "The increase in natural gas prices is a factor when you decide what to build," he said. "But it's only one factor. It's not the whole equation."

Today's high prices are the result of declining supplies of natural gas in the United States and Canada. As prices have climbed, wildcatters have hurried to drill more wells. But industry officials say that output has stagnated because the most abundant and accessible natural gas fields in the United States have been depleted. To boost domestic production, they argue, the government should allow exploration in areas that are now off-limits because of environmental concerns—the Rocky Mountains, the waters off the East and West coasts, and the Gulf of Mexico. . . .

Imported Liquid Natural Gas

The great hope of the natural gas industry lies in importing liquefied natural gas, known as LNG, a supercooled, supercondensed form of natural gas that can be shipped long distances in tankers. [Former] Federal Reserve Board chairman Alan Greenspan has repeatedly called for a major expansion of LNG imports. The United States now has four terminals designed to receive LNG from foreign producers and to convert the liquid back into gas. . . .

Residents of California, Maine, and Massachusetts are fighting proposed LNG terminals, however, arguing that the explosive fuel is an environmental risk and would invite terrorist attacks. Opposition intensified early [in 2004] after an Algerian LNG complex blew up during routine operations.

Under the most optimistic scenario, an increase in LNG imports could tame U.S. natural gas prices. "Post-2010, we can expect that substantial supplies of liquefied natural gas will be available to meet rising gas demand for electric generation," Piper predicts. "And the availability of LNG will discipline North American markets and bring prices down."

But others are skeptical. "We shouldn't be as comfortable as people seem to be that LNG is going to ride to the rescue," Makovich warns. American Electric Power CEO [Michael]

Morris agrees. "Why do we think that gas will tumble to our country, when the rest of the world's energy needs are increasing at a higher capacity than ours?" he asks. "I think it's a relatively myopic U.S. view—that the whole world is waiting to help us. I don't think they are."

Reinvestigating Nuclear Energy

[From 2004 to 2008], the Tennessee Valley Authority plans to spend $1.8 billion to refurbish one of its mothballed Browns Ferry nuclear power plants in Decatur, Ala. The TVA originally ordered the unit in 1974 but shut it and two sister plants down in 1984 because of safety concerns. Increased customer demand is driving the reopening.

The resurrection will mark the first time that a nuclear power plant has come on line since 1996, when the TVA's Watts Bar, Tenn., facility began producing power. Watts Bar was ordered before the Three Mile Island accident.

The nuclear industry is showing other signs of new life. Most promising are preliminary proposals by three industry consortia to build and operate new reactors in the United States. In May, the Energy Department gave one of those groups, led by the TVA, $2 million to study the feasibility of building a reactor at the TVA's Bellefonte site in northern Alabama. . . .

ANOTHER OPINION

On the Blacklist No More

After 25 years on the blacklist of America's energy sources, coal is poised to make a comeback, stoked by the demand for affordable electricity and the rising price of other fuels.

Mark Clayton, *Christian Science Monitor*, February 26, 2004.

Today, 103 nuclear power plants are operating in the United States, the vast majority of them located east of the Mississippi. When the NRC [Nuclear Regulatory Commission] originally licensed the plants in the 1970s and '80s, it granted them 40-year operating permits. Utilities have begun asking for 20-year extensions. The NRC has so far granted 23 of them and is considering another 19. The operators of nearly every U.S. reactor are expected to seek the 20-year extensions, according to Marvin Fertel, senior vice president of the Nuclear Energy Institute, the industry's trade association. Once built, nuclear power plants tend to be cheaper to run than natural gas or coal plants. . . .

A handful of electric utilities have been buying up most of the nation's nuclear plants, consolidating operations, and reducing management costs. Eight utilities now own a total of 61 nuclear plants.

Nuclear Risks

Nevertheless, from Wall Street's perspective, a huge cloud still hangs over the next generation of nuclear plants. Investors

Environmentalists advocate using renewable resources such as hydro and wind power, but it is questionable whether such sources can generate enough energy to power American society.

burned by construction cost overruns in the 1980s and '90s are not willing to sink more money into the industry until the next few plants are built, testified James Asselstine, managing director at Lehman Brothers, at a March congressional hearing. Investors "need a high degree of assurance that a new nuclear unit will be built at a predictable cost and on a dependable schedule," the former NRC commissioner said. "Until we gain this experience for the initial plants, both the industry and the financial community are likely to require some additional measures to mitigate construction completion and initial plant performance risk." . . .

Steve Kelley. © 2000 San Diego Union-Tribune. Copley News Service. Reproduced by permission.

Looking to Renewables

Thanks to [a government] tax credit, generators are harnessing wind power as never before in this country. Over the past five years, wind-power facilities have popped up in 30 states. "For most of the geographic areas of the U.S., wind is a cost-competitive option—with the production tax credit in place," said Randall Swisher, executive director of the American Wind Energy Association.

Environmentalists argue that the federal government could greatly boost the use of renewable energy by adopting a national renewable-energy standard that requires utility companies to generate part of their electricity from renewable sources. Fifteen states, including the president's home state of Texas, have adopted such standards. . . .

Swisher insists that . . . wind power could easily provide 6 percent of the nation's electricity by 2020. However, the Energy Information Administration projects that wind power, which supplied 0.3 percent of the nation's electricity in 2002, will generate only 1 percent by 2025. "The midterm prospects for wind power are uncertain, depending on future cost and performance, transmission availability, extension of the federal production tax credit [the credit was extended in October 2005] . . . other incentives, energy security, public interest, and environmental preferences," the EIA has reported.

The EIA expects renewable energy to provide up to 9 percent of the nation's electricity by 2025 but says most of that amount—5.3 percent—will come from hydroelectric dams. The largest increase in non-hydro renewable energy will come from biomass—wood and certain crops that are burned, either with coal or on their own, to produce electricity. According to the EIA, geothermal energy production will increase slightly over the next two decades, but solar technologies are not expected to begin making significant contributions to the U.S. grid-connected electricity supply by 2025. . . .

Keeping All Options Open

Industry executives insist that the nation needs to keep all of its power options open. "In the past decade, we have tilted heavily toward natural gas for new power plants," said David Owens, executive vice president of the Edison Electric Institute, which represents investor-owned utilities. "But in order to ensure a reliable and affordable supply of electricity, our industry must have access to a diverse range of fuels," he said. "New coal capacity already is being planned in a number of places. And at some point, we hope and expect that a new nuclear project will come to fruition."

Utilities and regulators find themselves trying to balance demand, environmental concerns, and expenses. And in the end, the bottom line often rules. "We have to keep in mind that the decisions we make at the end of the day affect our customers because they affect the price that we charge them," said PacifiCorp.'s Furman. "We're not only the stewards of the environment," he added. "We're the fiduciary stewards of our customers."

If natural gas prices remain high, and if proposed nuclear reactors continue to face daunting obstacles, the electricity industry will likely turn to coal to supply most of the 40 percent increase in power that Americans will demand by 2025—and will expect to have available with the flip of a switch.

Gasification of Coal Will Reduce Pollution Emissions

U.S. Department of Energy

In the following article, the U.S. Department of Energy contends that integrated gasification combined-cycle (IGCC) coal plants should deliver coal energy with fewer pollution emissions. That is, the burning of coal normally produces significant amounts of carbon dioxide (CO_2), sulfur oxides (SO_x), and nitrogen oxides (NO_x). IGCC technology, however, gasifies coal before it is burned, reducing many of these waste pollutants. The Department of Energy goes on to note that the remaining wastes can be captured and used to create syngas, a potential fuel. In addition, hydrogen, one of the byproducts of the burning process, can also be harnessed and used as an energy source.

Coal gasification offers one of the most versatile and clean ways to convert coal into electricity, hydrogen, and other valuable energy products.

The first coal gasification electric power plants are now operating commercially in the United States and in other nations, and many experts predict that coal gasification will be at the heart of the future generations of clean coal technology plants for several decades into the future. For example, at the core of the U.S. Department of Energy's *FutureGen* prototype power plant will be an advanced coal gasifier.

Rather than burning coal directly, gasification breaks down coal—or virtually any carbon-based feedstock—into its basic

U.S. Department of Energy, "Gasification Technology R&D," www.fossil.energy.gov.

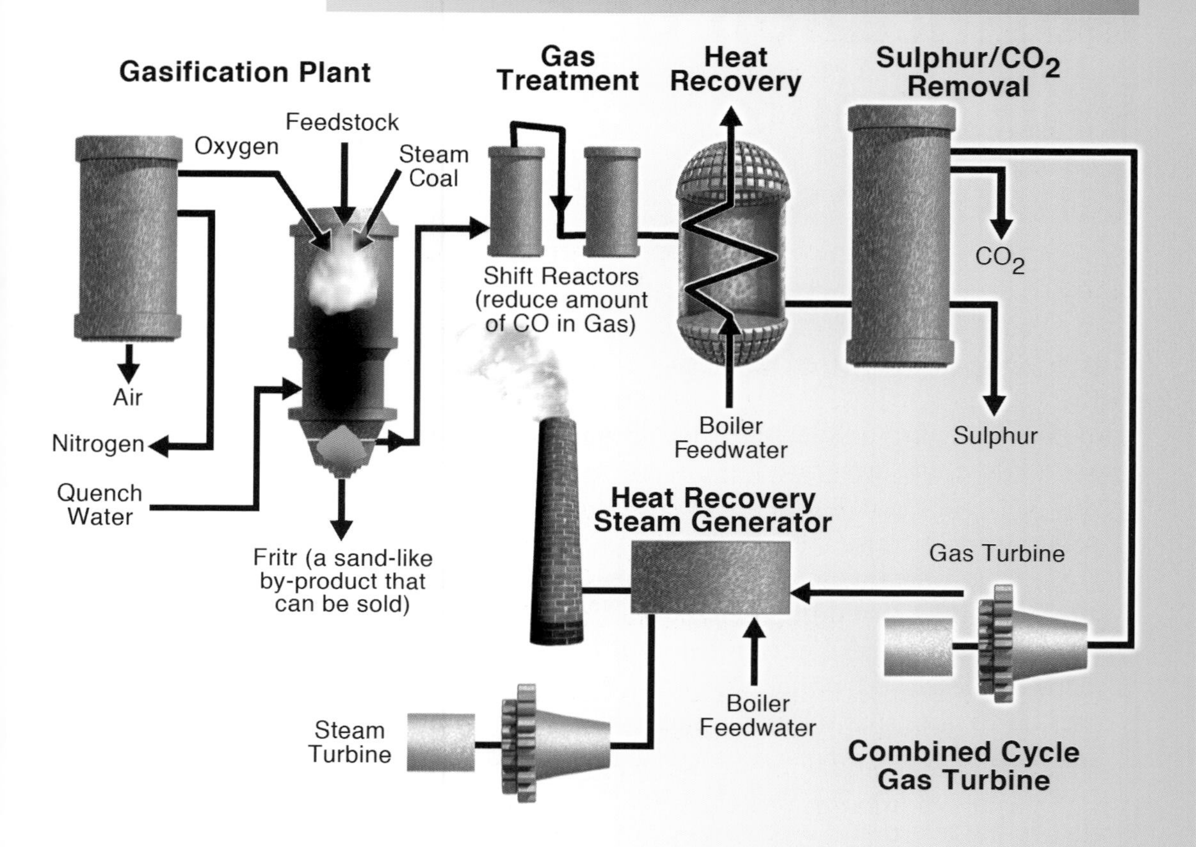

Source: Neil Wilkes, *Professional Engineering*, May 11, 2005.

chemical constituents. In a modern gasifier, coal is typically exposed to hot steam and carefully controlled amounts of air or oxygen under high temperatures and pressures. Under these conditions, carbon molecules in coal break apart, setting off chemical reactions that typically produce a mixture of carbon monoxide, hydrogen and other gaseous compounds.

Gasification, in fact, may be one of the best ways to produce clean-burning hydrogen for tomorrow's automobiles and power-generating fuel cells. Hydrogen and other coal gases can also be used to fuel power-generating turbines or as the chemical "building blocks" for a wide range of commercial products.

The Energy Department's Office of Fossil Energy is working

on coal gasifier advances that enhance efficiency, environmental performance, and reliability as well as expand the gasifier's flexibility to process a variety of coals and other feedstocks (including biomass and municipal/industrial wastes).

Environmental Benefits

The environmental benefits of gasification stem from the capability to achieve extremely low SO_x, NO_x and particulate emissions from burning coal-derived gases. Sulfur in coal, for example, emerges as hydrogen sulfide and can be captured by processes presently used in the chemical industry. In some methods, the sulfur can be extracted in either a liquid or solid form that can be sold commercially. In an integrated gasification combined-cycle plant, the syngas produced is virtually free of fuel-bound nitrogen. NO_x from the gas turbine is limited to thermal NO_x. Diluting the syngas allows for NO_x emissions as low as 15 parts per million. Selective Catalytic Reduction (SCR) can be used to reach levels comparable to firing with natural gas if required to meet more stringent emission levels, and other advanced control processes are being developed.

The Office of Fossil Energy is also exploring advanced syngas cleaning and conditioning processes that are even more effective in eliminating emissions from coal gasifiers. Multi-contaminant control processes are being developed that reduce pollutants to parts-per-billion levels and will be effective in cleaning mercury and other trace metals in addition to other impurities.

Coal gasification may offer a further environmental advantage in addressing concerns over the atmospheric buildup of greenhouse gases, such as carbon dioxide. If oxygen is used in a coal gasifier instead of air, carbon dioxide is emitted as a concentrated gas stream in syngas at high pressure. In this form, it can be captured and sequestered more easily and at lower costs. By contrast, when coal burns or is reacted in air, 80 percent of which is nitrogen, the resulting carbon dioxide is diluted and more costly to separate.

Efficiency gains are another benefit of coal gasification. In a typical coal combustion plant, heat from burning coal is used to boil water, making steam that drives a steam turbine-generator.

A coal gasification electric power plant rises into the sky. Coal gasification techniques can extract energy from coal with little environmental impact.

In some cases, only a third of the energy value of coal is actually converted into electricity by most combustion plants; the rest is lost as waste heat.

A coal gasification power plant, however, typically gets dual duty from the gases it produces. First, the coal gases, cleaned of impurities, are fired in a gas turbine—much like natural gas—to generate one source of electricity. The hot exhaust of the gas turbine is then used to generate steam for use in a more conventional steam turbine-generator. This dual source of electric power, called a "combined cycle," is much more efficient in converting coal's energy into usable electricity. The fuel efficiency of a coal gasification power plant in this type of combined cycle can be boosted to 50 percent or more.

Future concepts that incorporate a fuel cell or a fuel cell–gas turbine hybrid could achieve efficiencies nearly twice today's typical coal combustion plants. If any of the remaining waste heat can be channeled into process steam or heat, perhaps for nearby factories or district heating plants, the overall fuel use efficiency of future gasification plants could reach 70 to 80 percent.

Higher efficiencies translate into more economical electric power and potential savings for ratepayers. A more efficient plant also uses less fuel to generate power, meaning that less carbon dioxide is produced. In fact, coal gasification power processes under development by the Energy Department could cut the formation of carbon dioxide by 40 percent or more, per unit of output, compared to today's conventional coal-burning plant.

The capability to produce electricity, hydrogen, chemicals, or various combinations while eliminating nearly all air pollutants and potential greenhouse gas emissions makes coal gasification one of the most promising technologies for the energy plants of tomorrow.

Facts About Coal

Properties of Coal:

- Coal is a combustible sedimentary rock composed mostly of carbon and hydrocarbons. It is the most abundant fossil fuel in the United States.
- The energy stored in coal comes from plant matter that thrived hundreds of millions of years ago. This prehistoric plant matter was buried under swamps and then under layers of earth until the heat and pressure exerted by the various layers turned the carbon-filled plant matter into coal.

Properties of Coal as a Fuel:

- Coal is divided into four main ranks depending on the amounts and types of carbon it contains and on the amount of heat energy it can produce:
  - Lignite is the lowest rank of coal with the lowest energy content. Lignite has only a 25 to 35 percent carbon content; much of the rest of it is moisture. About 8 percent of the coal produced in the United States is lignite, and most of it comes from Texas and North Dakota. Lignite is mainly burned at power plants to generate electricity. The two types of lignite have energy densities that range from 14.6 to 19.3 megajoules/kilogram (mJ/kg).
  - Subbituminous coal has a higher heating value than lignite. Subbituminous coal typically contains 35 to 45 percent carbon. More than 40 percent of the coal produced in the United States is subbituminous. The four types of subbituminous coal have energy densities that range from 19.3 to 30.2 mJ/kg.
  - Bituminous coal contains two to three times the heating value of lignite. It has a carbon content of 45 to 86 percent. Half the coal mined in the United States is bituminous, making it the most abundant coal in the country.

Bituminous coal is used to generate electricity and in the production of steel. The four types of bituminous coal have energy densities that range from 30.2 to 32.5 mJ/kg.

- Anthracite contains 86 to 97 percent carbon and its heating value is slightly higher than bituminous coal. Anthracite is very rare in the United States. The only anthracite mines in the United States are located in northeastern Pennsylvania. The three types of anthracite coal have energy densities of 32.5 mJ/kg.

- Since 1976, coal has been the cheapest fuel for producing electricity in the United States.
- Coal is a fossil fuel, and when it is burned, it produces carbon dioxide (a greenhouse gas) and other pollutants. With newer "clean coal" technologies, coal emissions can be captured and stored, lessening or eliminating pollutants. This clean coal technology is expensive, and only a few demonstration coal plants have utilized capture and storage methods. Other clean coal technologies—such as scrubbers—are in use in many coal plants and have drastically reduced some dangerous emissions.

Coal Mining Methods:

- Surface mining: Most of the coal in the United States is mined near the surface (less than two hundred feet under the earth). These coal deposits are revealed through strip-mining, in which digging machines peel back the top layers of earth (overburden) to expose the coal.
- Underground mining: When coal deposits are hidden deep in the earth (sometimes up to one thousand feet below the surface), digging machines and miners must excavate mine shafts to reach the coal.

Coal Production Statistics:

- More than 20 percent of the world's coal is mined in the United States. Estimates suggest that as much as 35 percent of the world's coal deposits may lie in the United States.

- According to the Department of Energy, 99 million short tons (1 short ton = 2,000 lbs.) of coal were produced in the United States in March 2005. In 2004 a total of 1,111.5 million short tons were produced.
- The U.S. electric power sector consumed 92 million short tons of coal in January 2005. In 2004 a total of 1,015.1 million short tons were used to generate electric power in the United States.
- Another 89.2 million short tons were consumed by other U.S. industries (including coke plants, industrial plants, and residential and commercial heating facilities) in 2004.
- U.S. coal exports in January 2005 totaled 4 million short tons, 18 percent higher than exports in January 2004. In 2004 a total of 48 million short tons of coal were exported.
- U.S. coal imports in January 2005 totaled 2 million short tons, 15 percent higher than imports in January 2004. In 2004 a total of 27.3 million short tons of coal were imported.
- In 2003 5,406.27 million short tons of coal were produced worldwide. China (1,634.97 million), United States (1,069.5 million), India (403.12 million), Australia (373.36 million), Russia (294.03 million), South Africa (263.78 million), and Germany (229.10 million) produced the most coal.
- U.S. coal prices in 2004 rose from the previous year. Coal consumed by the electric power sector (where 92 percent of coal is used) cost $27.28 per short ton in 2004, an increase of 6 percent from 2003.
- Coal was used to generate 49.8 percent of U.S. electricity needs in 2004. Other energy sources that contributed to electricity generation included nuclear (19.9 percent), natural gas (17.9 percent), hydroelectric (6.5 percent), petroleum (3.0 percent), other renewables (2.3 percent), other gases (0.4 percent), and other sources (0.2 percent).

Coal Infrastructure:

- Coal is present beneath 458,600 square miles of the United States. That is about 13 percent of the country's land area.
- Thirty-eight states have coal deposits; twenty-seven states

have active coal mining operations. Wyoming mines the most coal, followed by West Virginia, Kentucky, Pennsylvania, and Texas.

- In 2004 there were 1,357 coal mines (both surface and underground) in the United States. They employed 73,801 workers in that year.
- In 2004 there were 55 plants producing synfuels from coal waste.

Clean Coal Technologies:

Various clean coal technologies (CCT) are used to reduce pollutants from the burning of coal. A few of the most notable are:

- Electrostatic precipitators (ESP) and fabric filters can remove up to 95.5 percent of particulate pollutants from coal smoke. An ESP creates a charged field in a coal furnace flue. Gas particles are ionized as they pass through the field and drawn toward collecting plates before they can escape the flue. ESPs are also effective at reducing mercury emissions. Alternatively, fabric filters block flues and catch particulate matter in tight meshes.
- Flue gas desulfurization (FGD) is a system that can remove up to 99 percent of sulfur emissions from burning coal. An FGD (also commonly called a "scrubber") uses limestone or a lime spray to react with the sulfur and draw it out of the coal gases. Scrubbers also remove some mercury emissions from coal smoke.
- Selective catalytic reduction (SCR) and selective noncatalytic reduction (SNCR) are used to remove nitrogen oxides (NO_x) from coal emissions. SCR reacts the NO_x with a catalyst and ammonia or urea in a postcombustion chamber. The reaction forms pure nitrogen and water. SNCR does not use a catalyst and injects the ammonia into the coal boiler directly to react with the nitrogen oxides.
- Low-NO_x burners are used to reduce nitrogen oxides at the source of combustion.
- Reburning is an experimental process in which part of the coal fuel is reburned in a second combustion chamber. In this

separate chamber, oxygen levels are kept low and nitrogen oxide emissions break apart before escaping out of the flue.

- Oxygen enrichment raises the temperature in a furnace, thus requiring less fuel to be burned. Using less fuel reduces nitrogen oxide emissions.
- Fluidized bed combustion (FBC) burns coal on a bed of heated particles that are suspended on a stream of air. At high temperatures, the air acts as a fluid, allowing for better mixing of burning elements and resulting in near-complete coal combustion. This reduces the amount of sulfur and nitrogen oxides that escape from the burning process.
- Supercritical and ultracritical coal furnaces burn coal at much higher temperatures and thus consume more of the energy trapped in the coal's carbon content. Less carbon escaping such furnaces reduces carbon dioxide (CO_2) emissions.
- Integrated gasification combined-cycle (IGCC) systems turn coal into a gas (syngas) that is cleaned of sulfur, nitrogen oxide, and carbon dioxide before it is burned.
- Carbon capture and storage (CCS) or carbon sequestration removes carbon dioxide from an IGCC coal-burning process and stores it for later use.

Glossary

anthracite: Any of three varieties of black, hard coal (called semianthracite, anthracite, and meta-anthracite) that has the least amount of moisture and highest heating value of all coals. It is highly sought after because it burns cleanly with little soot.

biomass: Biological crops or wastes harvested as an energy source. Biomass can be co-fired (burned together) with coal to reduce carbon dioxide (CO_2) emissions.

bituminous: Any of eight coal ranks (including subbituminous ranks) that has a black or dark brown color and contains a tarry substance called bitumen. Bituminous coals are used in power generation and in the production of steel.

carbon capture/sequestration: Also called carbon capture and storage [CCS]. The capture and storage of carbon dioxide (CO_2) and other greenhouse gases before they leave the coal-burning process and enter the atmosphere. The greenhouse gases are typically removed from the exhaust stream after coal combustion. The captured gases can be stored in special tanks or underground caverns, dissolved in saline reservoirs, or converted into solids.

catalyst: Any substance that speeds a chemical reaction. The catalyst is not part of the reaction nor is it used up in the reaction.

clean coal technologies: A number of processes used to reduce the amount of harmful pollutants (such as sulfur and carbon dioxide emissions) produced during the burning of coal. Some processes, such as the capture of carbon dioxide, occur close to the combustion stage of coal burning; other technologies, such as the use of flue scrubbers, remove impurities from coal smoke prior to its release into the atmosphere.

coal gasification: The transforming of coal into coal gas before it is burned to generate power. The gasification of coal significantly reduces impurities and pollutants associated with the direct burning of the fuel. Coal gasification is the driving force of integrated gasification combined-cycle power plants.

coal liquefaction: Sometimes called liquification. The process of converting solid coal into a liquid fuel such as gasoline, methanol, or diesel. The advantage of the process is to ease dependence on petroleum for these fuels. For coal liquefaction, either a direct or indirect process can be used. Indirect coal liquefaction first gasifies the coal, which removes sulfur and pollutants, and then synthesizes the fuels. Direct liquefaction dissolves pulverized coal in heavy oil filled with catalysts. The mixture is then fed into a reactor which produces fuel.

coke: A solid residue produced from low-sulfur, low-ash bituminous coal. Coke is formed through a coking process in which the moisture, gas, and tar are burned off coal, leaving behind a fused mass of ash and fixed carbon.

grade: An identifying aspect of coal. Grades reflect the amount of inorganic impurities, such as sulfur, in coal. The highest-grade coals have few impurities to interfere with the burning process. Low-grade coals have many impurities and release more pollutants, such as sulfur dioxide, when burned.

graphite: One of carbon's solid configurations. Graphite is used in heat-resistant technologies and in the making of lubricants and plastics.

integrated gasification combined-cycle (IGCC): A power plant combustion process that uses coal gasification technology to produce power. The coal gas combustion drives a gas turbine, and waste heat from the combustion process produces steam to drive a steam turbine. Both turbines then generate electricity. IGCC power plants are more expensive than traditional coal plants, but the gasification technology produces fewer pollutants.

kilowatt hour (kWh): A unit of energy equivalent to one thousand-watt-hours. One watt-hour equals one watt of power consumed in one hour of time. A one-hundred-watt light bulb, for example, would consume one hundred watts of power in one hour of use.

lignite: Also called brown coal, lignite is the lowest-ranked coal. It has the highest percentage of moisture (up to 45 percent) and the lowest heating value. It is used primarily in steam-to-electricity power generation.

mountaintop removal (MTR): A type of surface mining in which hills or mountains are clearcut of trees and then partially leveled with dynamite. The objective is to reach deposits of ore, mainly coal, that lie up to one thousand feet below the earth. The process radically changes the natural landscape.

polygeneration: An energy system in which an energy plant uses coal gasification to create syngas. The syngas is then used to produce energy in several ways. Some can be converted into a motor fuel or other fuels. The rest can be used to drive the power plant's gas turbine to produce electricity.

pulverized coal combustion (PCC): A clean coal technology in which coal is ground to a fine powder before being fed (along with combustible air) into a power plant's boiler. The pulverized coal burns more quickly, cleaner, and more efficiently than larger coal samples. PCC technology is most often used in conjunction with supercritical steam turbines.

rank: An identifying aspect of coal. Pressure and heat from long periods of burial progressively change the organic components of coal. The highest-rank coal has undergone the most extensive change. It retains the least amount of moisture and the largest percentage of fixed carbon, which determines its heating value. The ranks of coal (from highest to lowest heating value) are: meta-anthracite, anthracite, semianthracite, low-volatile bituminous, high-volatile A bituminous, high-volatile B bituminous, high-volatile C bituminous, subbituminous A, subbituminous B, subbituminous C, lignite A, and lignite B.

renewables: Energy resources that, unlike coal and other fossil fuels, are not depleted when used. Water power, solar power, and wind power are renewable energies.

seam: A deposit of ore, such as coal. Coal seams are typically horizontal bands of a certain depth and quality. If a coal seam lies near the earth's surface, it can be strip-mined. If the seam is buried far below the surface, it is commonly reached by underground mining.

slurry dam: A dam made of mine waste. The dam is used to retain a pond in which slurry, a mixture of solids and liquids from the cleaning and processing of coal, is deposited.

smelting: The process of changing the oxidation state of a metal ore, such as iron. Smelting commonly burns coke with the raw ore to remove oxygen from the metal compounds. The resulting pure metal can then be used in manufacturing.

strip-mining: The mining of ores, such as coal, that lie close to the earth's surface. Strip-mining involves the removal of the overburden—the top layer of soil and rock—to reach the ore seam.

supercritical steam generation: The pressurizing of water to a state at which there is no distinction between its gaseous and liquid phase. In a coal plant the resulting supercritical steam is fed through a turbine to generate power. The process reduces overall fuel consumption so that less coal is needed to provide the same power. Supercritical conditions also cut hazardous emissions by nearly half.

syngas: A contraction of the words *synthetic gas*. Syngas is primarily a mixture of carbon monoxide and hydrogen that is produced in coal gasification. Syngas can be stored and later converted to a combustible fuel or it can be used to drive a gas turbine in an integrated gasification combined-cycle system.

type: An identifying aspect of coal. The two types of coal are banded and nonbanded. Banded coal is composed of separate layers (bands) that contain mixtures of charcoal and plant debris. Nonbanded coal is smoother and is composed throughout of algae and plant spores.

underground mining: The extraction of ores from deep underground deposits. Conventional mining (also called room and pillar) involves digging out rooms and supporting the rock ceilings with pillars. Large underground complexes can be excavated using room and pillar mining. Longwall mining uses a machine with a moving ceiling support. As the machine digs out the ore, the ceiling support holds up the tunnel roof. When the ore is extracted, the machine moves on and allows the roof to collapse behind. If the ore deposit is closer to the surface, drift mining—or the digging of a single shaft to an ore seam—may be easier than conventional mining.

Chronology

B.C.

1000

Ancient Chinese may have used coal to smelt copper in the manufacture of coins.

A.D.

43–400s

During their invasion and occupation of Britain, the Romans discover coal and begin burning it for heat. When the Romans left England, the use of coal heat may have died out for seven centuries, as no written record mentions its use until the 1100s.

1000

Hopi Indians in present-day Arizona use coal to fire pottery.

1306

English smithies around London burn coal to replace decreasing wood stocks. Offended by the smell, nobles protest the fuel, and King Edward I subsequently bans its use. The ban is largely ignored.

1500s

England becomes the first Western nation to mine and burn coal on a grand scale. Much is used to feed the country's iron foundries. Coal smoke again becomes a civic problem.

1701

Coal is discovered by Huguenot settlers at Manakin, Virginia (near Richmond).

1712

British ironmonger Thomas Newcomen installs the first working model of his newly invented atmospheric engine at a coal mine to help pump water out of the mine shafts. The engine is fueled by coal.

1748
Virginia colonists at Manakin begin the first recorded U.S. coal mining operations.

1750s
Coal is discovered in areas that are now part of Kentucky, Ohio, Pennsylvania, and West Virginia.

1773
Scottish inventor James Watt improves on Thomas Newcomen's atmospheric engine and builds the first steam engine. Three years later, one of Watt's engines is installed as a water pump at a coal mine; another engine is used to operate the bellows in an iron foundry. The invention of the steam engine would soon revolutionize the manufacturing industry and kick off the Industrial Revolution.

1816
Baltimore, Maryland, becomes the first U.S. city to light streetlamps with gas generated from burning coal.

1830s
The first commercial locomotives are built in America. Originally designed to burn wood for power, the engines are quickly transformed to burn coal, which becomes the principal power source for all locomotives.

1848
The first U.S. coal miners' union is formed in Pennsylvania.

1860s
The U.S. steel industry furthers nationwide demand for coal.

1866
Strip-mining, or surface mining, is first practiced in the U.S. at coal mines near Danville, Illinois.

1880s
Cutting machines are introduced to relieve miners from the burdensome task of excavating coal by hand.

1882
American inventor and businessman Thomas Edison develops the first coal-fired electric power station in New York.

1890
The United Mine Workers of America (miners' union) is formed.

Late 1890s
The United States overtakes England as the world's largest coal producer.

1910
Steam shovels designed for excavating coal are used for surface mining.

1918
First use of pulverized coal in coal-fired power plants.

1929
Stock market crashes. Smart investors buy up bankrupt coal mines in anticipation of continued U.S. reliance on coal power.

1952
London, England, experiences a "Black Fog," a phenomenon in which the city's smoke is trapped under the atmosphere. The dense cloud of deadly gases, including sulfur dioxide, spreads throughout the city and kills around four thousand inhabitants. Four years later, Britain's Parliament bans the burning of coal in the city center and the air quality improves immediately.

1956
Railroads begin converting from coal to diesel fuel.

1960
Longwall mining with a roof-support machine is first practiced in the United States.

1961
Coal becomes the leading energy source for electric power in the United States.

1970
Federal Clean Air Act requires that U.S. air quality be significantly improved within five years. The target proves to be overly optimistic, but reductions in sulfur dioxide and other pollutants (especially from coal-fired power plants) remain a beneficial result of the legislation.

1973–1974
Middle Eastern oil embargo results in increased worldwide demand for U.S. coal.

1977
Federal Surface Mining Control and Reclamation Act (SMCRA) regulates the environmental impact of the coal-mining industry. Part of the legislation calls for the reclamation of mine lands that have been abandoned after use.

1982
Although coal supplies more than half of U.S. electrical energy needs, natural gas, hydropower, and nuclear energy are the dominant producers of electricity for home use.

1986
President Ronald Reagan initiates the Clean Coal Technology Program in response to Canadian concerns over acid rain generated from U.S. power plants. The program unites federal, state, and industrial leaders in developing and experimenting with various ways to make cleaner-burning, less-polluting coal plants.

1990
For the first time, U.S. coal production exceeds 1 billion tons in a single year. Clean Air Act of 1990 allows states to regulate their own pollution controls. The standards may be more stringent than the national standards set by the Environmental Protection Agency, but they may not be weaker.

1995
Five of the world's ten most polluted cities are located in China, which has been greatly expanding coal use to provide power to the nation's growing economy and population.

1996
U.S. Energy Policy Act of 1992 goes into effect and opens the electric utility market to competition between energy providers.

1997
At an annual international summit, several nations meet in Kyoto, Japan, and agree to reduce carbon dioxide emissions to specified levels between 2008 and 2112. The resulting Kyoto Protocol is to take effect in 2005. The United States and

Australia refuse to ratify the agreement, preferring to embark on their own plans to reduce domestic carbon dioxide emissions.

2002

President George W. Bush proposes the Clear Skies Act to reduce U.S. power plant emissions. The act utilizes a cap-and-trade strategy—a method by which polluting industries may trade unused pollution allotments to each other as long as neither exceeds a cap amount of pollution that can legally be spewed into the atmosphere. Since the pollution allotments are tradable, industries have a theoretical incentive to reduce pollution and make money through selling off unused allotments. The Congress has yet to approve the plan.

2005

U.S. Energy Policy Act of 2005 promotes clean coal technologies as a means of weaning the United States off imported oil and effectively addressing environmental issues.

For Further Reading

Books and Papers

Bruce Ackerman and William T. Hassler, *Clean Coal, Dirty Air: Or How the Clean Air Act Became a Multibillion-Dollar Bail-Out for High-Sulfur Coal Producers*. New Haven, CT: Yale University Press, 1981.

Barbara Freese, *Coal: A Human History*. Cambridge, MA: Perseus, 2003.

Ross Gelbspan, *Boiling Point: How Politicians, Big Oil and Coal, Journalists and Activists Are Fueling the Climate Crisis—And What We Can Do to Avert Disaster*. New York: Basic Books, 2004.

A.R Griffin, *Coalmining*. London: Longman, 1971.

Rita K. Hessley, John W. Reasoner, and John T. Riley, *Coal Science: An Introduction to Chemistry, Technology, and Utilization*. New York: John Wiley & Sons, 1986.

Brian Lewis, *Coal Mining in the Eighteenth and Nineteenth Centuries*. London: Longman, 1971.

Duane Lockard, *Coal: A Memoir and Critique*. Charlottesville: University Press of Virginia, 1998.

Bruce G. Miller, *Coal Energy Systems*. Boston: Academic Press, 2004.

Chad Montrie, *To Save the Land and People: A History of Opposition to Surface Coal Mining in Appalachia*. Chapel Hill: University of North Carolina Press, 2003.

National Research Council, *Coal: Energy for the Future*. Washington, DC: National Academies Press, 1995.

Dan Rottenberg, *In the Kingdom of Coal: An American Family and the Rock That Changed the World*. New York: Routledge, 2003.

Elspeth Thomson, *The Chinese Coal Industry: An Economic History*. New York: RoutledgeCurzon, 2003.

Matt Witt and Earl Dotter, *In Our Blood: Four Coal Mining Families*. Washington, DC: Highlander Research and Education Center, 1979.

World Coal Institute, *Clean Coal: Building a Future Through Technology*. London: World Coal Institute, 2004.

———, *Coal: Secure Energy*. London: World Coal Institute, October 2005

———, *The Coal Resource: A Comprehensive Overview of Coal*. London: World Coal Institute, May 2005.

Periodicals

Jeffrey Ball, "Kyoto Questioned as U.S. Moves on Coal," *Wall Street Journal*, December 6, 2005.

Lester R. Brown, "Coal: The United States Promotes While Canada and Europe Move Beyond," *Humanist*, vol. 64, no. 2, March/April 2004.

Mark Clayton, "America's New Coal Rush," *Christian Science Monitor*, February 26, 2004.

Economist, "Buried Losses," vol. 369, no. 8347, October 25, 2003.

———, "The Future Is Clean," vol. 372, no. 8391, September 4, 2004.

Scott Fields, "Coal Poised for a Comeback," *Environmental Health Perspectives*, vol. 112, no. 15, November 2004.

Michael Janofsky, "EPA Says Mercury Taints Fish Across U.S.," *New York Times*, August 25, 2004.

U.S. Department of Energy, Office of Fossil Energy (www.fe.doe.gov). The Department of Energy Web site provides information on coal technologies relating to the Clean Coal Power Initiative (CCPI). The CCPI was drafted by the administration of President George W. Bush, and it calls upon the na-

Dewitt John and Lee Paddock, "Clean Air and the Politics of Coal," *Issues in Science & Technology*, vol. 20, no. 2, Winter 2003/2004.

Margaret Kriz, "Coal: Not a Four-Letter Word," *National Journal*, vol. 36, no. 26, June 26, 2004.

Michael D. Lemonick et al., "How to Kick the Oil Habit," *Time*, vol. 166, no. 18, October 31, 2005.

Melanie Light, "Lasting Troubles in America's Coal Community," *Christian Science Monitor*, February 6, 2006.

David J. Lynch, "World's Deadliest Coal Mines Power China's Progress," *USA Today*, July 8, 2003.

Steve Maich, "Will Coal Bury Kyoto?" *Maclean's*, vol. 118, no. 3, January 17, 2005.

Robert Peltier, "A Pollution-Free Coal Plant," *Power*, vol. 147, no. 4, May 2003.

Otis Port, "All Fired Up Over Clean Coal," *Business Week*, February 16, 2004.

Kit R. Roane, "Digging for Black Gold," *U.S. News & World Report*, vol. 139, no. 23, December 19, 2005.

Simon Romero, "Fuel of the Future? Some Say Coal," *New York Times*, November 20, 2004.

Brian K. Schimmoller, "Coal Gasification: Striking While the Iron Is Hot," *Power Engineering*, vol. 109, no. 3, March 2005.

Larry J.Schweiger, "Global Warming: It's Time to Act," *National Wildlife*, vol. 44, no. 1, December 2005/January 2006.

Rebecca Smith, "Industry Cheers Push for Cleaner-Coal Technologies," *Wall Street Journal*, February 2, 2006.

Index

air pollution
coal as source of, 41–42
electricity and, 77
from power plants, 53–54
Alliance to Save Energy, 55
anthracite coal, 31, 39
Asselstine, James, 86

Barnett, Joe, 64, 67
Barnett, Judith, 64
Benner, Katie, 71
bituminous coal, 39
Bonds, Julia, 61, 62–64, 65, 69
Boulton, Matthew, 21
Britain
coal burning in, 14
history of coal in, 26–27, 39
leading iron producer, 25
British thermal units (Btus), 31, 39
Browner, Carol, 57
Bush, George W., 42
Bush administration, 62
attempts to regulate greenhouse gas, 15–16
reductions in CO_2 proposed by, 78
spending on coal research, 71–72

Canterberry, Pauline, 67
carbon dioxide (CO_2), 12
from electricity generation, 77
emission of
from coal-fired electrical plants, 41
from coal use, 74
global warming and, 73
projected increase in, 12
carbon sequestration, 74
cost of, 75
Carey, Mike, 72, 74
cast iron, 25
China, 59
Church, Lynne H., 81
Clayton, Mark, 84
Clean Air Act (1970), 15, 42, 56, 76
Clean Coal Power Initiative (CCPI), 16
clean coal technologies, 45
cost of, 72–74
see also coal gasification
Clear Skies program, 42
coal
conversion of, 46
emissions, 52–53
energy value of, 31
grades of, 32
history of, 10
in Britain, 26–27
industrial uses of, 40
origins of, 28–29, 37–38
processing of, 39
projected demand for, 45
ranks of, 30–31

United States. Its coal data Web page contains several charts and graphs covering coal stocks, imports, exports, distribution, and consumption since the mid-twentieth century. The EIA also gathers information on the state of international coal supply and demand.

reserves of, 38
in U.S., 12
societal impact of, 43–44
top countries producing, 16
transition from, in Europe, 55
types of, 29–30
Coal: A Human History (Freese), 19
coal fires, 48
coal gasification, 45–47, 89–90
benefits and drawbacks, 47–48
cost of, 72–74
environmental benefits, 91, 92
fuel efficiency of, 93
coal mining
environmental impacts of, 42–43
increase in, 42–46
methods of, 32, 33
strip mining, 34, 38–39
underground mining, 34–36
Coal River Mountain Watch, 62
coke, 25
continuous miner, 36
Cooper, Roger, 82

Department of Energy, U.S. (DOE), 89
developing nations
coal as key to economic growth, 17
use of outdated technology by, 42

Edison Electric Institute, 88
Edward I (king of England), 14
efficiency standards, for household appliances, 55
electrical generation
coal-fired
annual deaths from, 78
increase in use of, 40
mercury emissions from, 52
process of, 46
from renewable sources, 78–79, 87
sources of, 11, 76, 82
Electric Power Research Institute, 59
Electric Power Supply Association, 81
energy demands, world, projections of, 13
Energy Information Administration (EIA), 71, 72, 79, 87
Environmental Protection Agency (EPA)
on deaths from coal-fired plant emissions, 78
on emissions from electricity industry, 77
on mercury in fish, 51–52
mercury standards set by, 56
regulation of power plant emissions by, 15

Faroe Islands study, 58
Fertel, Marvin, 84
Food and Drug Administration (FDA), 58
Franklin, Benjamin, 21

Freese, Barbara, 19
FutureGen initiative, 74

geothermal energy, 87
Gerard, Jack, 80
Griffin, A.R., 25

Hamilton, Dave, 73–74, 75
Hattam, Jennifer, 60
health risks
 from air pollution, 53–54, 78
 to coal minors, 43–44
 of mercury exposure, 50–51
Hessley, Rita K., 10, 28
household appliances, 55

Industrial Revolution, 10, 27, 43
International Energy Agency (IAE), on predicted world energy demands, 13
iron smelting, 24

Kerry, John, 72
Kriz, Margaret, 76
Kyoto Protocol, 15

Larsen, Janet, 50
lignite coal, 31, 39
liquefied natural gas (LNG), 83–84
longwall mining, 35–36

Makovich, Lawrence, 80, 83
mercury
 from coal-fired electrical plants, 41
  plants leading in, 54
  states leading in, 51
 health risks of, 50–51
 U.S. emissions of, 58
metaanthracite coal, 32
methane gas, 12–13
methylmercury, 52
Michaels, Patrick J., 58
Miller, Mary, 67
Morey, Mark, 72, 73

National Gas Supply Association, 82
natural gas
 electrical generation by, 76
 supply of, vs. coal supply, 80
Natural Resources Defense Council (NRDC), 57
Newcomen engine, 20, 22, 24
New York Times (newspaper), 17
nitrogen oxides, 41
nuclear power
 electrical generation by, 76
 operating plants, in U.S., 84
 renaissance of, 78
 risks of, 85–86
Nuclear Regulatory Commission (NRC), 84

Owens, David, 88

peat, 38
Peltier, Robert, 56
Piper, Steve, 80
power plants
 annual air pollution deaths from, 53–54

coal-fired, in U.S., 17
nuclear, in U.S., 84
see also electrical generation

Reasoner, John W., 10, 28
renewable energy, 78–79
Riley, John T., 10, 28
Romero, Simon, 17
room-and-pillar mining, 34–35

Schanzer, Dave, 75
Schlager, Neil, 37
Seychelles Island study, 59
Sierra (magazine), 60
slurry dams, 64
solar energy, 87
strip mining (surface mining), 34, 38–39
alternatives to, 69
in West Virginia, 61–62
areas suitable for, 63
environmental destruction from, 64–66
sulfur, 32
sulfur dioxides, 32
coal-fired electrical plants and, 41
from electricity generation, 77
surface mining. *See* strip mining
Swisher, Randall, 87

tailings, 48
Tennessee Valley Authority (TVA), 84

United Mine Workers of America (UMWA), 69
United States
annual coal consumption of, 10
electricity generation in
from renewables, 87
sources of, 11
Kyoto Protocol rejected by, 15
map of coal deposits in, 12
nuclear power plants in, 84
U.S. Geological Survey, 80
U.S. Public Interest Research Group, 52

Watt, James, 19–24
Watt steam pump, 23
Weisblatt, Jayne, 37
West Virginia
strip mining in, 61–62
areas suitable for, 63
impact on environment, 64–66
politics and, 66–67
Whitesville, West Virginia, 60–61
Wicks, Roger, 13
Wilkinson, John, 21
wind power, 79, 87
World Coal Institute, 10, 17, 28–29
wrought iron, 25

Picture Credits

Cover: © Michael S. Yamashita/CORBIS
© Bettmann/CORBIS, 11, 20, 26
© Bob Sacha/CORBIS, 13, 44, 49
© Charles E. Rotkin/CORBIS, 65, 68
© Charles Philip Cangialosi/CORBIS, 53
© Craig Aurness, CORBIS, 18
© George Steinmetz/CORBIS, 35, 61
© James L. Amos/CORBIS, 81
© John Noble/CORBIS, 57
© Lester Lefkowitz/CORBIS, 14
© Paul A. Souders/CORBIS, 42
© Paul Hardy/CORBIS, 77
Photos.com, 79, 85 (both),
© Richard Klune/CORBIS, 70
© Roger Ressmeyer, 73, 92
© Tim Wright/CORBIS, 30
Victor Habbick Visions, 12, 16, 22–23, 29, 33, 40, 46, 51, 54, 63, 66, 74, 82, 90

About the Editor

David M. Haugen holds a master's degree in English from the University of Washington. He has served as the managing editor of Greenhaven Press and as a general editor for Lucent Books. He now works as a freelance writer and editor. He is the author of more than thirty young-adult, nonfiction titles.